REA: THE TEST PREP AP® TEACHERS RECOMMEND

2nd Edition

AP® WORLD HISTORY
CRASH COURSE®

By Jay P. Harmon, M.Ed.

Research & Education Association
Visit our website at: www.rea.com

Research & Education Association
61 Ethel Road West
Piscataway, New Jersey 08854
E-mail: info@rea.com

AP® WORLD HISTORY CRASH COURSE®

Printed in the United States of America

Library of Congress Control Number 2016948513

ISBN-13: 978-0-7386-1218-8
ISBN-10: 0-7386-1218-9

Cover image: istockphoto.com/arekmalang

A17

AP WORLD HISTORY CRASH COURSE TABLE OF CONTENTS

PART I

INTRODUCTION

PART II

CHRONOLOGICAL REVIEW

PERIOD 1: Technological and Environmental
Transformations, to c. 600 BCE

PERIOD 2: Organization and Reorganization of
Human Societies, c. 600 BCE—c. 600 CE

KEY CONCEPTS AND THEMES

TEST-TAKING STRATEGIES

Online Practice Exam .... *www.rea.com/studycenter*

ABOUT THIS BOOK

REA's *AP World History Crash Course* is designed for the last-minute studier or any AP student who wants a quick refresher on the course. The *Crash Course* is based on the latest changes to the AP World History course curriculum and exam.

Written by an expert who has been closely involved with the AP World History course since its beginning, our easy-to-read format gives you a rapid survey of the major concepts and strategies in AP World History. The targeted review chapters will prepare you for the exam by focusing on important topics frequently seen on the AP World History exam.

Unlike other test preps, REA's *AP World History Crash Course* gives you a review specifically designed to zero in on the "big ideas" tested on the exam. Each chapter highlights the important themes and terms to keep in mind as you prepare.

Part I gives you the Keys for Success, so you can tackle the exam with confidence. It also lists important terms that you absolutely, positively must know. Part II is a Chronological Review based on the most current AP World History curriculum. It presents essential information you need to know.

Part III reveals the Key Concepts and Themes of the AP World History framework to remind you of the important overall developments throughout World History. Part IV explains the format of the AP World History exam and offers test-taking strategies to conquer the multiple-choice and short answer questions, the Document-Based Question, and the long essay.

No matter how or when you prepare for the AP World History exam, REA's **Crash Course** will show you how to study efficiently and strategically, so you can boost your score!

To check your test readiness for the AP World History exam, either before or after studying this **Crash Course**, take REA's **FREE online practice exam**, that has been fully updated to align with the 2017 exam changes. To access your practice exam, visit the online REA Study Center at *www.rea.com/studycenter* and follow the on-screen instructions. This true-to-format test features automatic scoring, detailed explanations of all answers, and diagnostic score reporting that will help you identify your strengths and weaknesses so you'll be ready on exam day!

Good luck on your AP World History exam!

ABOUT OUR AUTHOR

Jay P. Harmon earned his B.S. and M.Ed. from Louisiana State University, Baton Rouge, Louisiana. He began his teaching career in 1982 and has taught in public and private schools in Louisiana and Texas. Mr. Harmon has taught AP European History, AP United States History, and AP World History.

He was an exam essay reader in AP European History and AP United States History and was a table leader and question leader in AP World History from the exam's beginning in 2002 until 2015. He served on the AP World History Test Development Committee and founded the College Board's Electronic Discussion Groups (EDGs) in AP United States History, AP European History, and AP World History. His AP European History and AP World History websites (*www.harmonhistory.com*) have been go-to resources for students and teachers for more than a decade.

Beginning in 1998, Mr. Harmon served as a consultant to the College Board, holding AP workshops and summer institutes in the United States and abroad. He has also contributed to the development of several history textbooks.

I would like to extend my special thanks to my wife, Monica, my sons, Joey and Christopher, the faculty and staff at Houston Christian High School, my A4 and B2 classes, and Ga Young Seo and Katherine Kovach for their support on this exciting project.

ACKNOWLEDGMENTS

In addition to our author, we would like to thank Larry B. Kling, Vice President, Editorial, for his overall guidance; Pam Weston, Publisher, for setting the quality standards for production integrity and managing the publication to completion; and Diane Goldschmidt, Managing Editor, for editorial project management.

We would also like to extend special thanks to Emily Millians for technically reviewing the manuscript, Marianne L'Abbate for copyediting, and Kathy Caratozzolo of Caragraphics for typesetting this edition.

PART I
INTRODUCTION

Eight Keys to Success
on the AP World History Exam

"So . . . what do I need to know?" you're asking yourself. Oh, not much .... only more than ten *thousand* years of history. Wait, don't throw away this book and run screaming from the room. First, take a deep breath and examine the facts: More than 200,000 high school students just like you will take the AP World History exam this school year and about half of them will earn college credit. *Why not you?* You're clearly a clever and motivated person—after all, you're reading this *Crash Course* study guide.

Good news: You don't have to know *everything* from the beginnings of humans to the early twenty-first century to do well on the AP World History exam. By studying efficiently and strategically, you can get college credit and add that special AP-credit sparkle to your transcripts. Use the following keys to success:

1.   Know the Content and Format of the Exam

The AP World History exam content is broken down into the following chronological categories. The column "Weight on Test (Percent)" refers to the percentage of the exam that will come from each historical period.

	Historical Periods	Weight on Test (Percent)
Period 1	Technological and Environmental Transformations, to c. 600 BCE	5

Period 2	Organization and Reorganization of Human Societies, c. 600 BCE to c. 600 CE	15
	Historical Periods	**Weight on Test (Percent)**
Period 3	Regional and Interregional Interactions, c. 600 CE to c. 1450	20
Period 4	Global Interactions: c.1450 to c. 1750	20
Period 5	Industrialization and Global Integration, c. 1750 to c. 1900	20
Period 6	Accelerating Global Change and Realignments, c. 1900 to the present	20

By studying the chart and knowing that there are 55 multiple-choice questions, you might deduce that there aren't many questions from Period 1. This helps you focus your plan of study. In addition, though the AP World History exam states that it covers human history "to the present," the reality is that you won't be expected to know much beyond the end of the Cold War in the early 1990s.

The latest updates to AP World History exam content and structure can be found at *http://apcentral.collegeboard.org*.

2. Know Your Competition

Don't be intimidated by your competition—you have an advantage over most of them by paying attention to the advice in this book. Over 70 percent of students who take the AP World History exam are sophomores, and most of them are taking their first AP exam. The next biggest group is composed of seniors, then juniors and freshmen. You already read that about *half* of all AP World History test-takers pass the exam and get college credit by scoring a 3, 4, or 5 on a scale of 1 to 5.

Caution: Don't get overconfident and think you've got it made just because you've read this far. Taking an AP exam and receiving college credit takes *a lot* of focused work. You need serious, organized preparation to be successful.

3. **Know How the Exam Is Scored**

The AP World History exam has two main parts: Section 1, which consists of multiple-choice questions and short answer questions, and Section 2, which has two essay questions. The multiple-choice portion is scored by machine, contains 55 questions, and must be completed in 55 minutes. It is worth 40% of the total exam score. Just like any multiple-choice test, you will answer some questions very quickly and others will take more time. When the multiple-choice part of the exam is over, you will then answer four short-answer questions in 50 minutes, worth 20% of the total exam score. Then you will have a short break and return for the essay part of the exam. Bring a snack and a bottle of water for the break.

In Section 2 of the exam, you will write two essays: a document-based question (DBQ) and a long essay. You will have 90 minutes to complete both essays. Each essay is read and scored by a trained AP World History teacher or a World History college professor. In June, AP World History essay readers meet to score all the essays over the course of about a week. Then your essay scores—which comprise 40% of the exam—are added to your Section 1 scores to arrive at your final AP score.

You'll find more tips about tackling the multiple-choice, short answer, and the essays in the discussions about test-taking strategies in Part IV of this book.

4. **Know What Your Final Score Means**

The College Board uses a formula to rank your combined multiple-choice, short-answer, and free-response score into five categories:

5 = Extremely Well Qualified

4 = Well Qualified

3 = Qualified

2 = Possibly Qualified

1 = No Recommendation

A passing grade on all AP exams is a 3. Only about 11 percent of AP World History test takers earn a score of 5, but keep reading—the scoring range is more generous than you probably think. If you get about half of the exam's multiple-choice questions right and score average on the short-answer and essay parts of the exam, you should reach a "3." That doesn't mean the exam is easy—the opposite is true. Remember only about 11% of test takers score a 5—an indication of how challenging the test actually is.

In AP World History, about half of all exam takers make a "3" or better. Many colleges give course credit with a score of 3; other colleges take nothing below a 4, while still others give college credit only for 5s. Find out the AP policies of the colleges you are interested in attending. And be aware that colleges and universities can change their AP acceptance policies whenever they want. Stay up-to-date by checking college AP policies on their websites.

5. **Know How AP World History Is Different from Traditional World History**

You might think that history is history, but AP World History is different from traditional approaches: Learning lists of "Kings and Wars" or "The West and the Rest" doesn't cut it. The AP World History test developers want you to see the big picture. They want you to make connections across the globe and across time and to analyze common human experiences like migration, trade, religion, politics, and society. Think of it this way: Studying AP World History is like learning American History. You don't examine the histories of 50 individual states—instead you learn about the important themes, people, and events of *American* history. The same idea applies to AP World History: think globally, not nationally, and in most cases you'll do well. A big tip: If your World History textbook doesn't say "Advanced Placement" or "AP" on the cover, look at the introduction to see if the authors discuss concepts like global history and making connections between civilizations across time and place. If not, you may need to find a different textbook that explains history in these ways.

6.   **Know What You Don't Need to Know**

Nobody expects you to know everything about World History in order to do well on the AP exam. First, AP World History is about the *human* experience, so you won't need to know when the Big Bang was or what killed the dinosaurs. AP World History is more about the big picture than the little details, so you also don't need to memorize all the monarchs of England, the battles of the Crimean War, or the name of Alexander the Great's horse (Bucephalus, by the way).

Second, 95 percent of the AP World History exam covers 600 BCE to the present, so you don't need to memorize the entire Code of Hammurabi from Babylon, but you *do* need to know the importance of codes of law from early civilizations.

Third, what is "BCE" anyway? That's fast becoming the way historians denote the traditional term "BC." It stands for "Before the Common Era," so naturally, the Common Era, or "CE," is how the AP World History exam refers to the traditional "AD." (In case you're wondering, you live in the twenty-first century, no matter which terminology you prefer!)

7.   **Know How to Use This *Crash Course* to Build a Plan for Success on the AP World History Exam**

This *Crash Course* is based on a careful study of the trends in both course study and exam content.

In Part I, you'll be introduced to the AP World History course and exam. In Chapter 2, you'll find a list of key terms and concepts that you *must* know for success.

In Part II—Chapters 3 through 19—you will find chronological reviews of important political, economic, and social trends and connections in world history. These reviews are based on the current AP World History Curriculum Framework—the College Board's guide for teachers and exam creators.

Part III, Key Concepts and Themes (Chapters 20 through 26), includes helpful charts and tables designed to show you connections across time and place.

Finally, Part IV (Chapters 27 through 31) prepares you to take the exam by giving you insider test-taking strategies for the multiple-choice questions, the short-answer questions, the Document-Based Question (DBQ), and the long-essay question.

8. **Know How to Supplement This *Crash Course***

This *Crash Course* contains what you need to do well on the AP World History exam, but an exceptional student like yourself will want to make use of everything that can help. Visit the College Board's AP Central website for essay questions and sample responses. Keep in mind that exams released prior to 2016 are not the same format as the 2017 exam, but can be used as a guide for essay topics.

Key Terms and Concepts

Period 1:   Technological and Environmental Transformations, to c. 600 BCE

1.   **Hunting-Foraging Bands**

Before the development of agriculture, nomadic peoples around the world lived in small groups that were often related to each other. They hunted game and collected wild or undomesticated plants for food. These people are also known as hunter-gatherer groups. Technology included bows and arrows, Clovis points (large stone arrowheads) and spears. While those tools may not sound much like technology to us, in their day, those tools were vital in assisting humans in the hunt. The very survival of hunting-foraging bands depended on finding adequate food supplies from wild game and plants. Most of the individuals in these groups practiced a form of religion called *animism*. See details below.

2.   **Neolithic Revolutions**

First in the Middle East around 8000 BCE and later in other regions (see River Valley Civilizations), hunter-foragers settled in areas with a steady water supply and good soil, planted seeds in the ground on purpose—agriculture—and lived in permanent buildings in villages. In the Neolithic Revolutions, irrigation of crops was developed and animals, such as dogs, cats, cattle, and horses, were domesticated to aid with hunting, transportation, and agriculture, and/or function as a food supply. One result of closer contact with animals was increased exchanges of diseases to and from people.

3.   **River Valley Civilizations**

The River Valley Civilizations are those first places where Neolithic Revolutions occurred. Mesopotamia in the Middle East ("Mesopotamia" means "between the rivers"); the Nile Valley in North Africa (the Egyptians); the Indus River Valley in South Asia; and the Shang in the Yellow, or Huang He, River Valley in East Asia were among the earliest known river valleys where agriculture first began. The classic definition of "civilization" means "a city" and these early civilizations also built the first buildings made of stone or brick, and placed them together to form the villages, which developed into cities. See Urbanization.

4.   **Pastoralism**

While some people were settling into cities, others raised domesticated animals but did not develop agriculture, so they remained on the move. They were known as *pastoralists*. In moving with their herds, they spread information about other groups and developments in technology. Call them "agents of change." Pastoralists emerged in parts of Africa, Europe, and Asia around the same time as the Neolithic Revolution. One example of a pastoral group that is still functioning in the twenty-first century are the Mongols of East Asia.

5.   **Urbanization**

Small villages in River Valley Civilizations often grew into larger cities, and those cities became important centers of government, trade, and religion. Urban areas saw the development of specialization of jobs, such as scribes or merchants; social levels, such as elites and slaves; and gender roles, such as expectations that men would usually be government leaders and members of the military and women would usually engage in domestic functions like cooking, sewing, and child-rearing. Counting and writing systems began in cities as a means of keeping records of stored food and other goods. One of the first writing systems was *cuneiform* from Mesopotamia. Religious temples like Ziggurats in Mesopotamia are examples of monumental architecture that developed in early cities. Some examples of early cities in Eurasia are Sumer in Mesopotamia, Catal Huyuk in Turkey, and Mohenjo Daro and Harappa in South Asia's Indus River Valley. In

the Americas, the Olmec civilization developed cities in Mesoamerica by 1600 BCE, and the Chavin civilization, along the coast
of modern-day Peru, built urban centers by 900 BCE.

6.   **Early Empires**

Over time, more cities developed in the River Valley Civilizations
and were united under a ruler, or king, who claimed his power
was derived from the gods. The Babylonians in Mesopotamia
were one early empire that conquered rival cities by force and
put them under one code of law. A very important example of a
written early law code was the Code of Hammurabi, from Babylon, about 1750 BCE. The Egyptians in North Africa established a
large and long-lasting empire that, at its peak, stretched along
the Nile River from modern Sudan to the Mediterranean coast,
west into modern Libya and northeast into modern Lebanon.

7.   **Animism/Polytheism**

The earliest-known form of religion, *animism*, sees gods in nature
(worshipping the sun, for example). It was popular among
hunting-foraging bands. Polytheism ("many gods") differs from
animism in that gods in polytheism have specific names and
duties. The Greek god Apollo, for example, was the god "in
charge" of the sun.

8.   **Monotheism**

Monotheism is the belief in one god. The Hebrews of Southwest
Asia practiced one of the earliest known monotheistic religions,
Judaism. This feature set them apart from their neighbors and
made them unique in early history. Another early monotheistic
faith, from Persia in Central Asia, was Zoroastrianism.

**Period 2:   Organization and Reorganization of Human
            Societies, c. 600 BCE to c. 600 CE**

9.   **Classical Era**

Historians have labeled the years c. 600 BCE to c. 600 CE the
Classical Era. During this period classical empires such as the

Greek and Roman civilizations in the Mediterranean region, the Han Dynasty in East Asia, and the Maurya and Gupta empires in South Asia rose in political, social, and economic power, and then fell. Other important classical civilizations of this era include the Persians in Central Asia and the Mayans in Mesoamerica.

10. **Hinduism**

The earliest known organized religion, with written codes of the faith and a class of religious leaders (priests), Hinduism was centered in South Asia. Its beliefs were influenced by Indo-European groups who migrated into the region from western areas near the Caspian Sea. Hindu teachings supported the caste system that greatly influenced the political and social structure of South Asia.

11. **Buddhism**

A "reform" of Hinduism was begun by Prince Siddhartha Gautama c. 500 BCE, who became the Buddha ("Enlightened One"). Unlike Hinduism, Buddhism supported spiritual equality and missionary activity. Buddhism spread far from its origins in South Asia into Southeast and East Asia along trade routes.

12. **Confucianism**

Based on the teachings of Kong Fuzi (Confucius) in China, c. 500 BCE. He established clearly defined codes of behavior, and gender and family duties. Confucius's teachings were a philosophy, not a religion dedicated to a deity. Over time, however, Neo-Confucianism emerged, which included aspects of Buddhism and Daoism, and promised eternal reward for faithfulness to Confucius's teachings.

13. **Christianity**

Like Buddhism was to Hinduism, Christianity was a reform of an existing religion, Judaism. Jesus taught eternal salvation through the belief that he was the Jewish Messiah, sent by God to save humanity from eternal punishment. Jesus named his disciple Peter as his first successor; this act represents one political difference with Islam's hierarchy (see No. 25). Over time, missionaries spread

Jesus' gospel ("good news") throughout the Roman Empire and beyond. Christianity, Buddhism, and Islam spread globally and are the religions with the most followers today.

14.   Han Empire

Han + Rome — same time

East Asia's Han Empire existed around the same time as the Roman Empire. In fact, they traded with each other. The Han was one of the largest empires of the classical era and, in terms of technology, was far ahead of other civilizations of the same era.

15.   Mandate of Heaven

The Mandate of Heaven reflected the belief that the emperor in China would stay in power as long as the heavens were satisfied with his rule. If the emperor's family line (a dynasty) died out or was overthrown, it was a sign that the emperor had lost his mandate. Although many dynasties rose and fell in China over the centuries, the Mandate of Heaven was a continuity that added stability to society.

16.   Chinese Examination System

The Chinese examination system was a political feature of Chinese empires beginning with the Han dynasty and lasting until the early twentieth century. Scholar-bureaucrats took state-sponsored exams in order to become government scribes and serve in other capacities to help emperors run the affairs of state. In this system, it was possible—but rare—for even low-born citizens to rise to political prominence.

17.   Mediterranean Civilizations

"Mediterranean civilizations" is a term used in AP World History to describe the classical Greek and Roman civilizations. The Romans borrowed so much of their political, social, and economic culture from the Greeks that, from a global perspective, historians find it convenient to combine the two.

18.   Hellenism

In the fourth century BCE, Alexander the Great conquered the Persian Empire and put his social and political Greek stamp on his short-lived empire, which stretched from Egypt to India. "Hellenistic" culture is a blend of Greek and local styles. One example of Hellenistic art is a Buddha statue made in unmistakable Greek style, with lifelike features and flowing robes.

19. **Maurya/Gupta Empires**

These classical empires in South Asia were geographically extensive and powerful empires. The Mauryan Empire existed from c. 320 to c. 185 BCE; the Gupta Empire lasted from c. 320 CE to c. 550 CE. Another later powerful South Asian empire was the Mughal (see 46 below). These empires were exceptions to the trend of political fragmentation in South Asian history. During most of its existence, India had many regional leaders, not one unified empire, as these others were.

20. **Bantu Migrations**

The Bantu migrations are the most-often cited sub-Saharan event in Africa that occurred over much of the Classical era. Beginning in central Africa c. 1000 BCE to c. 500 CE, Bantu-speaking peoples migrated south and east over many centuries, spreading a common language base and metal-working technology.

21. **The Silk Roads**

A must-know trade route, the Silk Roads connected East Asia to northern India and central Asia and, indirectly, to the Mediterranean region, West Africa, and northern Europe. Silk, tea, spices, horses, and technology were carried westward along camel and horse caravan routes. Chinese goods and technology made their way into southwest Asia, Africa, and Europe along these routes.

22. **Indian Ocean Trade Network**

Connected to the Silk Roads, the Indian Ocean trade network was just as important, but with routes over water. African, Arab, Jewish, and Chinese, both Muslim and Christian, merchants carried religion (especially Buddhism and Islam) and exchanged silver, cotton, spices, and many other items across the Indian Ocean.

23.   **Fall of Classical Empires**

Beginning c. 200 CE, all three major classical empires declined and fell. First to go was the Han Dynasty in China (c. 220 CE), followed by the western Roman Empire (476 CE), and finally the Gupta Empire in India in the mid-sixth century CE. All three fell from internal pressures, such as peasant revolts, and external pressures, such as invading nomads and imported diseases.

Period 3:   Regional and Interregional Interactions, c. 600 CE to c. 1450

24.   **Trans-Sahara Trade**

Trade of goods, people, and faith across North Africa's Sahara desert peaked from the eighth century CE to the 1500s. Camels were the main mode of transportation. Gold, salt, animal hides, and slaves were among the main items transported out of Africa to points east and north. Muslim merchants imported camels into the region; they also brought along their faith in Islam, which spread rapidly into North and West Africa. Three important West African trade centers along these trade routes were Djenne, Goa, and Timbuktu.

25.   **Islam**

First preached in Arabia in the seventh century CE by the prophet Muhammad, a merchant who preached monotheism. Islam ("submission") united multiple polytheistic Arab tribes into a common faith. By the mid-700s, it had spread rapidly via trade routes out of southwest Asia across North Africa to Spain and eastward into northern India and Central Asia. Muslim merchants carried Islam into Southeast and East Asia.

26.   **Caliphate**

Unlike Christianity, Islam had no clear rules of succession after Muhammad. Culturally, Islam united many peoples, but politically, it fragmented into regional states called *caliphates*, each led by a caliph. The AP World History exam asks more questions

about the Abbasid caliphate than the Umayyad or Fatamid caliphates.

27.   Crusades

A series of Christian versus Muslim military campaigns for the
"holy land" in Southwest Asia and for parts of the Byzantine
empire. The major Crusades occurred sporadically from 1100 to
1300. Politically, European Christians failed to permanently re-
gain much land, but culturally they reacquired much knowledge
through contact with Muslims, including the reintroduction of
Greek and Roman learning into Europe, which in turn sparked
the Renaissance.

28.   Dar al-Islam

Basically, Dar al-Islam is "everywhere Islam is" across Afro-Eurasia.
In the era c. 600–1450, this term described the territory extending from Spain and Northwest Africa all the way to South and
Southeast Asia. Dar al-Islam was not a unified political empire
but a large region where Islamic faith and culture was dominant.

29.   Diffusion of Religions

In the era c. 600–c. 1450, three religions spread far outside their
places of origin: Christianity, Buddhism, and Islam. Buddhism
and Christianity were spread by missionary monks. Conversions
to Christianity and Islam were also done by "sword mission,"
meaning by force. Like Buddhism, Islam was also spread peacefully by merchants along trade routes.

30.   Byzantine Empire

Although the western Roman Empire fell in 476 CE, the eastern
portion, headquartered in Constantinople, continued for another
thousand years. (Byzantine comes from the original name of
Constantinople, *Byzantium*.) This empire had major economic,
social, and political influence over southern and eastern Europe,
the Eastern Mediterranean, and Southwest Asia.

31. **Tang and Song Dynasties**

The Tang and Song dynasties were two of the most famous dynasties in all of Chinese history, not just in the era c. 600– c. 1450. Under the Tang and Song dynasties, China had the world's largest population, the most advanced technology, and the most splendid cities. (How to remember them? "Drink some Tang and sing a Song.")

32. **Sinification**

Think of "sinification" as the "Chinese-ification" of Japan, Korea, and Southeast Asia. China was such a powerful neighbor that it was inevitable that nearby countries would follow its political, social, and economic examples.

33. **Mongols**

"Agents of change" or "an unstoppable tide of horror"—both definitions are right. Mongol forces invaded south China and rode west all the way into Russia and Southwest Asia in the thirteenth and fourteenth centuries. After brutal conquest, they established a *Pax Mongolica*: peace and trade throughout their territories.

34. **Black Death**

The Black Death is probably history's most infamous disease. Historians believe it may have originated along the trade routes near the Black Sea. It spread east and west during the age of the Mongol conquests, killing millions. For example, in the mid-four-teenth century, the Black Death wiped out as much as one-third of the population of western Europe.

35. **Mayan States**

The Mayan States were centered in Mesoamerica (southern Mexico and parts of Central America). Like the Egyptians, the Mayan civilization featured pyramids, large cities, a written language, and a complex society. Its height was during the American classical era of 250–900 CE. Tikal was an important Mayan city.

36. **Coerced Labor**

"Coerced labor" includes slavery, serfdom, the corvee (government-required labor on public works projects), and indentured servitude. Forms of coerced labor existed across all civilizations and time periods. For the era c. 600–c. 1450, European serfdom is a common example of coerced labor found on the AP World History exam.

37. **Feudalism**

In western Europe and in Japan in this era, many people served as agricultural workers for landowners, a system called feudalism. In both areas, regional armies fought over land rights at the bidding of their local lords. In Europe, elite warriors were called *knights*; in Japan, they were known as *samurai*.

38. **Zheng He**

Representing the power of the Ming dynasty, the explorer Zheng He led enormous expeditions that included huge treasure ships and thousands of sailors, and crossed the Indian Ocean and traveled to the Spice Islands of Southeast Asia in the early fifteenth century.

Period 4: Global Interactions, c. 1450 to c. 1750

39. **Inca Empire**

Centered in the Andes Mountains in western South America, the Inca civilization was built on previous cultures in their region. Their empire extended along the western coast, a result of both conquest and diplomacy. Its peak of influence was in the fifteenth century; it declined rapidly when Spanish conquistadors arrived in the early sixteenth century.

40. **European Explorations**

Seeking an increase in the trade of spices, silk, and other goods from East and Southeast Asia, kings from new European nations sent ships around Africa into the Indian Ocean and also across the Atlantic Ocean. Led by Portugal, then Spain, France, England, and Holland, these explorers initiated the first truly global contacts and ushered in the rise of European influence around the world.

41.   Columbian Exchange

Columbus's expeditions to the Americas triggered exchanges of plants, animals, technology, and diseases on a worldwide level. This term is a key definition in the global scope of AP World History.

42.   Atlantic World

The Atlantic World encompasses the people, politics, religions, goods, and ideas that crossed back and forth over the Atlantic after Columbus's journeys connected Europe, Africa, and North and South America. This term is especially important in the years c. 1450–c. 1900.

43.   Mercantilism

Europe's new worldwide power because of the Columbian Exchange included mercantilism as an example of economic nationalism. Under mercantilist policies, nations developed colonies in the Americas and Asia and used them to provide raw materials such as sugar, furs, silver, and lumber. These products were then processed and sold by companies from the owner (mercantilist) nation all over the world. Each mercantilist nation competed with the others to amass and keep as many colonies as it could as a sign of economic and political power.

44.   Atlantic Slave Trade

European mercantilists needed many laborers to work on the large sugar plantations of the Caribbean. These laborers were found mainly in West Africa, and millions were seized and shipped across the Atlantic in the so-called *middle passage*. As a result, great demographic changes occurred in both Africa and the New World.

45.   Encomienda System

The encomienda system was a Spanish practice that was used in Spain's American colonies and in the Philippines. Spanish settlers were granted tracts of land and were permitted to use the native people already living on that land as indentured servants.

46. Mughal Empire

The Mughal Empire was a Muslim empire in South Asia that lasted from the mid-sixteenth to the mid-nineteenth centuries. One of its famous leaders was Akbar. Religious tolerance was one of its features. The Taj Mahal was built during the Mughal reign. Mughal leaders claimed to be descended from the Mongols, which is where the name "Mughal" comes from.

47. Syncretism in Religions

A "world-class" religion must be flexible enough to adapt to local customs as it spreads. Many examples of a world-class religion exist: when Buddhism spread into Southeast Asia, the Buddha became a god-like provider of eternal salvation; as Islam spread into parts of South Asia, it adopted some Hindu features and turned toward mysticism with Sufism; some forms of Christianity in the New World adopted traditional gods and made them part of the pantheon of saints.

48. Printing Press

Developed in China c. 500 CE, printing technology moved along trade routes, arriving in Germany by the fifteenth century, where it spread rapidly into many other areas of Europe. The short structure of Western alphabets was a great benefit in printing. In contrast, the Chinese written language contained thousands of word characters, making printing more challenging.

49. Ottoman Empire

A Muslim empire that expanded from Southwest Asia into parts of North Africa and Eastern Europe, the Ottoman Empire began in the thirteenth century and lasted until the early twentieth century. Ottoman Turks ruled this large empire. The Ottoman Empire was an important political, social, and economic conduit for Western Europe, Africa, and East Asia for many centuries.

**Period 5:   Industrialization and Global Integration,
              c. 1750 to c. 1900**

50.   **Industrialization**

The Industrial Revolution began in England in the mid-eighteenth century and was a major part of the West's enormous social changes and economic and political expansions in the nineteenth century. It marks the shift from slow hand-made to rapid machine-made production. Industrialization spread to Russia, South and East Asia, and North and South America by the end of the nineteenth century.

51.   **Enlightenment**

Like the Industrial Revolution, the Enlightenment was a western European development in this era that had tremendous effects on a global scale. Having its foundations in scientific study and intellectual reason, its basic tenets included individual rights such as freedom of speech and participation in government. It greatly influenced the American and French Revolutions, which in turn inspired political revolutions around the world.

52.   **Capitalism**

An offshoot of the Enlightenment and strongly attached to the Industrial Revolution, capitalism is an economic system based on individual economic development. Private investors use their money (capital) to invest in potentially profitable activities. Adam Smith was an important English proponent of capitalism. The industrialized nations of the early twenty-first century hang their economic hats on capitalism to varying degrees.

53.   **Marxism**

In the mid-nineteenth century, Karl Marx proposed an alternative to capitalism in an attempt to close the gap between the rich and poor in industrial western Europe and one day, he hoped, the world. In Marxism, the many poor unite and overthrow the few rich, and establish a political and economic system where the government controls production and labor to the benefit of all.

54. **Nationalism**

Belief that a group of people with similar cultural backgrounds rightly belong together in one nation. It became popular in western Europe in the nineteenth century and spread globally, leading to many wars for independence, most notably in Latin America.

55. **Age of Revolutions**

During the mid-nineteenth-century "Age of Isms" in western Europe (see Nos. 52 through 54), many revolutions seeking political and social change occurred, inspired by the ideas of the Enlightenment and the French Revolution. In Latin America, most countries successfully revolted against European political control in this era.

56. **Imperialism**

In the nineteenth century, western Europe's economic and industrial power made it the world's strongest political force, and its nations accumulated colonies all over the world. Russia, Japan, and the United States also participated. A famous quotation that reflects the national pride that accompanied imperialist expansion was, "The sun never sets on the British Empire." At its peak, Britain claimed colonies in half of Africa and much of South and Southeast Asia.

57. **Social Darwinism**

Connected to strong nationalist ideas, Europe's political and industrial superiority led to the belief that it was socially and morally superior to the peoples it conquered. Charles Darwin's "survival of the fittest" scientific theory in the animal world was applied to non-European peoples around the globe.

58. **Resistance to Western Hegemony**

Local resistance to European imperialism was widespread. Examples include the following: The Chinese government attempted to stop England's importation of opium; anti-colonial rebellions broke out in Africa; and in India, the National Congress promoted self-rule.

59.   Meiji Restoration

In an attempt to compete with the West's industrial and political power, Japan embarked upon the Meiji Restoration, reorganizing its government in the late nineteenth century. The emperor's power was reestablished, and Japan purposefully westernized its industrial base and even its society.

60.   Nineteenth-Century Migrations

The Industrial Revolution included improvements in transportation that made ocean travel safer and cheaper. Pushed by revolutions and poor living conditions, and pulled by stories of opportunities, millions of people, especially Europeans but also South and East Asians, migrated to North and South America in the nineteenth century.

61.   Indentured Servitude

Part of the nineteenth-century migrations was a result of the end of slavery in areas under Western control. Thousands of South Asians migrated to South Africa and the Caribbean as agricultural indentured servants. East Asians were also employed as indentured servants in the Americas.

62.   Open Door Policy

At the beginning of the twentieth century, the United States flexed its new global muscles by proposing that the United States, Japan, and the European powers share open access to trade with China, and the other powers accepted the U.S. plan. The weak government in China was unable to resist the economic and political influence of these nations. The Open Door Policy is widely regarded as a sign of the "arrival" of the United States in global affairs.

63.   "Second" Industrial Revolution

The "first" Industrial Revolution involved the mechanization of agriculture and textiles, but in the last half of the nineteenth century, its focus changed to innovations in electricity (telephone and radio), chemistry (fertilizers), transportation (cars and airplanes), and steel (skyscrapers and modern weapons). These developments continued to influence the rapid social and economic changes in the West into the twentieth century.

Period 6: Accelerating Global Change and Realignments, c. 1900 to the Present

64. The World Wars

The first half of the twentieth century saw two enormous wars among the "Great Powers" of Europe, Asia, and the United States. These wars were caused in part by massive military production made possible by the Industrial Revolution and by global competition for territories during the Age of Imperialism. In an AP World History context, World Wars I and II can be seen as one long, global war with a 20-year break between the two. The results of the wars were the decline of western Europe and the rise of the power of the United States and Soviet Union in the second half of the twentieth century.

65. The Great Depression

Between the two World Wars, a global economic disaster struck the industrialized nations around the world. By the end of World War I, the United States had the world's largest economy; when it failed in the late 1920s, the economies of much of the rest of the world, which were already reeling from the effects of World War I, were severely affected. Two major results were authoritarian governments (see No. 66) and World War II.

66. Authoritarianism

One result of the catastrophe of World War I was a rejection of democratic forms of government in parts of Europe and Asia, namely, Germany, Italy, Russia, and Japan. Single-party rule led by a strongman with dictatorial powers was thought to be a more efficient system than democracy. Communism and fascism were the best-known examples of such governmental systems. The growing military aggression of the fascist governments was a cause of World War II.

67. **Communism**

Communism was originally proposed by Karl Marx from Germany in the mid-nineteenth century and put in place by Vladimir Lenin in Russia in the early twentieth century. In this economic and political system of socialism, the government (the state) attempts to direct the economy and to provide services for all. Authoritarianism was often the method of rule in communist systems. Communism spread around the globe in the twentieth century and competed directly with capitalist societies.

68. **Decolonization**

A major global development after World War II was Europe's process of getting rid of its colonial empires around the world. Colonies in South Asia, Southeast Asia, and Africa regained their independence, but they often faced many significant social, economic, and political challenges.

69. **Partition**

The largest British colony, India, partitioned itself, or split up, along religious lines when it gained independence in 1947, forming India (with a Hindu majority) and Pakistan. In 1971, East Pakistan separated from Pakistan to become Bangladesh (both with Muslim majorities). For many decades afterward, Pakistan and India were major rivals in the region of South Asia.

70. **Cold War**

The dominant global conflict after World War II, the Cold War was conducted between the United States (and its allies) and the Soviet Union (and its allies). The aim for each side was to keep the other from increasing its political and economic influence around the world. It was called the Cold War because the two sides did everything to prepare for a real hot war (with real weapons) except actually fight each other directly. Massive accumulation of nuclear and other forms of weapons threatened mutually assured destruction, but when the Soviet Union fell apart in the late twentieth century, the Cold War ended.

71. Multinational or Transnational Corporation

A multinational or transnational corporation does business in more than one country. The British and Dutch East India companies of the eighteenth century were early examples, but it was after World War II in the twentieth century that this business model became common. Today, Exxon Mobil, Toyota, and General Electric are prominent examples of multinational and/or transnational corporations.

72. Pacific Rim

In the second half of the twentieth century, strong economies developed on both sides of the Pacific. Although the United States was a major economic power in the region, the term usually refers to the economies based in nations such as China, Japan, Australia, South Korea, and Singapore.

73. Chinese Revolutions

In the early twentieth century, a revolution in China against the emperor led to a limited democracy. After World War II, communists led by Mao Zedong overthrew that government. Vast social, political, and economic changes resulted. Until the late twentieth century, communist China was relatively isolated from global economic involvement, but after Mao's death, China opened its economic system to allow capitalist development, and its economy boomed.

74. Apartheid

Apartheid was a political and social policy in South Africa in the mid-twentieth century that separated whites and blacks and that granted the white minority many rights that the black majority was denied. The apartheid policy was reversed in the late twentieth century after decades of global pressure, and majority rule was established.

75. Feminism

Although its roots extended back to the Enlightenment (see No. 51), feminism was largely a twentieth-century movement dedicated to increasing the political, social, and economic rights of women. It began in Western democracies and expanded to include much of the world by century's end. Counterexamples persisted in parts of the Middle East, Africa, and Asia.

76. Globalization

"Globalization" describes the "shrinking world" that resulted from increased economic and communications connections. While the term *could* be applied to world systems after Columbus's voyages (see No. 41) or to the Age of Imperialism (see No. 56), it became especially popular in the late twentieth century. Not everyone was content with the process of globalization.

77. Historiography

The AP World History exam defines historiography as "historical interpretation." Historiography is the study of the study of history—or the different ways that historians interpret the past at different times. This is important to an AP World History student because developing the skills to find a point of view and to discern multiple historical perspectives is a vital part of the course and the exam. See Chapter 22 for insights into developing these important AP World History skills.

78. Periodization

"Periodization" means knowing when things happened. You won't need to know exact dates but you do need to know in what period major people and events occurred. For example, you need to know that the Roman and Han empires ended about the same time, toward the end of the era c. 600 BCE—c. 600 CE, and that the Mayan states fell in the next era, around the 9th century. A good way to keep track is to make charts labeled, "To c. 600 BCE," "c. 600 BCE—c. 600 CE," and so on. Fill in the charts with important political, social, economic, cultural and environmental trends. It also might help to label a map to accompany each chart.

World Regions in AP World History

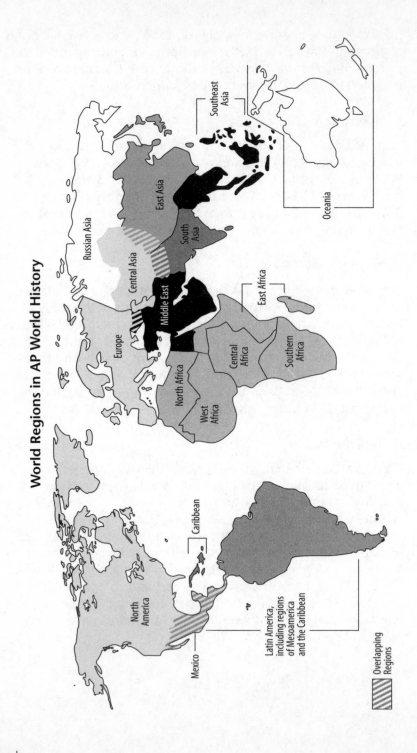

PART II
CHRONOLOGICAL
Review

PERIOD 1

TECHNOLOGICAL AND ENVIRONMENTAL TRANSFORMATIONS

To c. 600 BCE

Pre-History to c. 600 BCE

Preparing for the AP World History exam does not mean you have to know all history "from the dawn of time" until the present. Instead, the exam focuses on important developments over time in different places. As you move through this book, you will see an increase in the connections between civilizations as they encounter each other. You will also notice that as history approaches the early twenty-first century, time "slows down" in the AP World History curriculum. This chapter covers the most amount of time, but it contains the least amount of detail. By the time you reach your study of the twentieth century, you will see much more detail covered for the least amount of time— just 100 years.

I. Peopling the Earth

A. The Paleolithic or Old Stone Age era (c. 250,000 BCE– c. 8000 BCE)

1. Archaeological evidence indicates that early humans migrated from Africa to Europe, Asia, Australia, and the Americas, usually in small hunting-foraging bands that survived by hunting animals and gathering edible plants. These groups usually had family connections.

2. In this era, humans learned to use tools made from stone and wood. Tools included the spear, the bow and arrow, the club, and the stone axe. Paintings on cave walls from about 17,000 years ago in France show people hunting with these types of tools.

3. Humans started religious practices in this era.

   i. Archaeological evidence indicates that religions were usually animistic; that is, they attributed sacred powers to events in nature. Abundant examples of ceremonial burials have been found. These burials indicate that the dead in this era weren't just left to the wild animals. Instead they were carefully placed in graves with flowers and other objects, showing that the living expected their dead to carry on into an afterlife.

   ii. Another example of religious belief is that archaeologists have found many examples from this era of small statues of deities made from stone and clay.
      ↳ Gods / Goddesses

4. Trade of goods and technology occurred between bands of hunter-foragers.

   i. As groups encountered each other, they may have fought over nearby herds of animals and at other times, hunted together for animals, grains, and fruit. In these encounters, they exchanged weapon- and tool-making technology and possibly religious beliefs.

Test Tip

It is important that you understand the geography of the peopling of the Earth, so be sure to study maps that show the migrations of early humans in this era.

started in Africa!

II. The Neolithic Revolution (also called the Agricultural Revolution) (c. 8000 BCE)

A. About 8000 BCE, humans began to plant crops in areas with rich soil and abundant water, usually found in river valleys.

1. Starting in Southwest Asia, in an area called Mesopotamia ("between the rivers"), people deliberately planted seeds and harvested their crops instead of constantly roaming around looking for fruits, grains, and nuts.

2. Planting seeds in the ground on purpose is agriculture. Many people in this era began to stay in areas with fertile

land and build permanent shelters near their crops. Others continued their hunting-foraging ways.

3. Humans also settled along the Nile River in North Africa, the Yellow (Huang) River Valley in East Asia, and the Indus River Valley in South Asia. Other early agricultural civilizations included those in Mesoamerica (southern Mexico and nearby areas) and in the Andes mountains of modern-day Peru. ⟶ Chavin

B. Note that the Neolithic Revolution did not occur globally and concurrently, meaning that people didn't start planting crops all over the world at exactly the same time.

1. Agriculture developed in China about 2000 years after Mesopotamia.

2. In the Andes and Mesoamerica, agriculture occurred in about the year 2500 BCE.

Test Tip

This divergence of dates of the Neolithic Revolution is an example of the difficulties historians have in assigning periods in world history. Thus, the writers of the AP World History exam expect you to understand the concept of periodization. (See Chapter 23.)

C. Animals were domesticated during this period as well.

1. Humans tamed wild animals and used them for protection, for food, and also to help in the hunt. Dogs, cats, goats, sheep, cattle, horses, chickens, and pigs were the most important domesticated animals in Afro-Eurasia.

2. In the Americas, horses didn't exist until Europeans brought them during the late fifteenth century CE. However, in South America, the Chavin in the Andes mountain region domesticated llamas and alpacas.

3. Because of closer contact with animals, diseases were increasingly transferred between humans and animals.

D. Technological developments increased food production.

1. Wooden plows, wheels, sickles, traps, clay pots, and large woven baskets allowed for more efficient planting and harvesting of food—this led to more food being available, which in turn led to an increase in population growth.

2. Humans also learned to dig irrigation canals that brought water from the rivers to their crops, increasing yet again the amount of food produced.

3. Humans figured out how to melt metals like iron, gold, silver, tin, and copper to create cooking utensils like cups and pots, religious figurines, and weapons.

   i. Bronze, a mixture of tin and copper, was greatly valued because it could hold a sharp edge, unlike most early manufactured metals.

   ii. Iron was also a hard metal that, once refined, was used to make weapons and plow tips. — Hittites

E. Because more food was available, people lived longer and had more children, who in turn had more children, and so on.

1. This increase in population is one factor in the development of the world's first cities.

2. Storing food became an important function—keeping account of how much food was available led to the first writing systems.

F. Societies developed specialization of labor and social structures.

1. With the Agricultural Revolution's steady food supply, people tended to stay in one place.

   i. This led to a specialization of work tasks and jobs, such as craftspeople, warriors, religious leaders, and government officials (like kings and scribes).

      ➤ Craftspeople, such as construction workers, built storage facilities for food reserves;

> ➤ Warriors protected their food supplies from outside attacks and sometimes attacked other cities to take their food;

> ➤ Religious leaders asked their gods to supply good food harvests;

> ➤ Scribes kept records of how much food was on hand; and

> ➤ Kings told them all what to do.

III. Early Urban Societies

A. Cities with permanent building structures developed out of agricultural settlements.

    1. *Civilization* is a term many historians use to describe societies that have cities.

        i. The first cities, in Mesopotamia and the Nile Valley, developed roughly six thousand years ago. They had buildings made both of stone and of a human invention—sun-dried bricks. They discovered that by stacking bricks into an arch, multi-story buildings could be created. *Arch* is the root word of *architecture*.

        ii. Tall buildings of religious importance in Mesopotamia were called *ziggurats*, and in Egypt, they were called *pyramids*.

        iii. Elites (royalty) had palaces built for themselves. (The AP World History exam calls such buildings "monumental structures.") Kings commissioned statues, carvings on buildings and walls (also called *bas relief*), and elaborate tapestries and paintings to decorate their palaces.

B. Cities had both political and religious leaders who usually worked together to maintain social order.

    1. Sometimes the same people held both positions because it was difficult to question the authority of a leader who was also a god.

    i.   To pay for construction of protective city walls, kings imposed taxes on businesses and individuals.

    ii. To keep records of stored grain supplies, writing systems developed, like *cuneiform* in Mesopotamia and *hieroglyphics* in Egypt.

> ➤ The roots of the English alphabet came from the Phoenicians of Southwest Asia, who passed it to the Greeks, then the Romans, and so on.

C. Legal codes were written and enforced by the courts to maintain order in the ever-crowded cities.

    1. The most well-known early legal code, the Code of Hammurabi, came from Mesopotamia. Its rules, such as "an eye for an eye," were first established in Southwest Asia.

D. Over time, cities that had close proximity to each other, a common language, and common religious beliefs began to unite to form early empires.

    1. These empires were led by kings who almost always claimed that their authority came from the gods.

    2. The Babylonians and Hittites of Mesopotamia and the Egyptians are examples of early empires.

    3. Empires were built and expanded by conquering people who lived beyond the borders of the empire.

    4. Over the centuries, the patterns of empire-building established in this era were repeated often in every region and time period.

Test Tip

For the AP World History exam, it is important to be familiar with political and social features of the following empires: those in Mesopotamia, Egypt, the Shang in China, the Harappan and Mohenjo-Daro in the Indus Valley, the Olmecs in Mesoamerica, and the Chavin in Andean South America. You must also be able to locate them on a map.

E. The first literature emerged in the era of the early civilizations. Written stories explaining the world's creation and the meaning of life was a common theme.

   1. From Mesopotamia, *The Epic of Gilgamesh* addressed questions about life and death and explored human relationships.

   2. *The Rig Veda* (from the Indus Valley) and *The Book of the Dead* (from Egypt) sought to explain religious themes such as the origin of the Earth and its peoples and the destiny of humans after this life ends.

F. Nonsettled groups—pastoralists—transferred technology, goods, and ideas among settled societies.

   1. *Pastoralists* were nomadic people who herded domesticated animals such as sheep, horses, goats, and/or cattle in central Asia, the Arabian Peninsula, and parts of Africa. They did not participate in agriculture like the settled peoples of the cities.

   2. Pastoralists fostered connections between settled areas and were agents of change across long distances, sometimes peacefully, other times through raids designed to take the stored materials found in the cities.

G. Religions developed in this era carried over into later periods.

   1. Hinduism, which developed in the Indus River Valley, is probably the world's oldest religion.

      i.   It was influenced by the Aryan peoples of Central Asia.

      ii. The *Vedas* are the religious texts of Hinduism.

      iii. The Hindu faith adheres to the belief in one overall god-spirit, but believes that it reveals itself to humanity in many forms.

   2. Although most religions from this era were polytheistic (believing in many gods or many representations of god), two stand out as unique in their monotheism:

      i.   The Hebrew faith from Southwest Asia; and

      ii. Zoroastrianism out of Central Asia.

H. Social pyramids emerged.

1. Elites, such as rulers and religious leaders, were at the top of the pyramid; craftspeople, merchants, and laborers were in the middle; and slaves were on the bottom.

2. Social and political systems tended to be patriarchal, with men holding power in governments, religions, and families. Women attained political power through marriage or by supervising their young ruling sons.

Test Tip

The material in this chapter accounts for only 5 percent of the AP World History exam, so plan your study time accordingly.

PERIOD 2

ORGANIZATION AND REORGANIZATION OF HUMAN SOCIETIES

C. 600 BCE – C. 600 CE

Religious and Cultural Developments
c. 600 BCE – c. 600 CE

The years c. 600 BCE to c. 600 CE are known as the Classical Era. Political and social trends from this era had great influence on later generations and still influence societies today. Many religions that developed in this era had long-term effects in places far from their points of origin. Faith offered comfort in difficult times, created social stability and structure, and provided authority to political leaders. Other cultural foundations of civilizations were established during this era as well, such as Greek theater, Confucianism, religious art and literature, and Mediterranean architecture.

I. Faiths Develop

A. Belief systems continued to develop from earlier eras; others emerged and spread.

1. The monotheistic Hebrew faith in southwest Asia was scattered (the Jewish diaspora) to the eastern Mediterranean region and into central Asia by the Assyrians in approximately 600 BCE and by the Romans around 70 CE. Jewish merchants carried the faith to small pockets of communities in major trade cities in Europe and in South and East Asia.

2. In South Asia, Hinduism established a spiritual and social caste system that created a long-term foundation for civilizations there.

   i. Hindu beliefs were influenced by concepts from the Vedic religions brought in by Indo-European groups and from local traditions. For centuries, beliefs were passed on through oral traditions, but later they were recorded in sacred texts, including the *Vedas* and the *Upanishads*.

ii. Hinduism teaches that there are many manifestations of the Great Soul of the Universe; To westerners, Hinduism appears to be both polytheistic and monotheistic.

➤ Unlike Christianity or Buddhism, there is no single founder of Hinduism. It developed over many years in South Asia out of a blending of various religious traditions, many of which were brought in from outside the region.

➤ The caste system was an important part of the culture in India at this time. All living things participated in the caste system.

— Through cycles of birth, death, and reincarnation, believers hoped to elevate their souls to the highest level of spirituality or *moksah*, when they become one with Brahman, the Great Soul.

— The process could take many hundreds or thousands of lifetimes.

— A soul may move up or down the ladder toward unity with Brahman depending on one's deeds and sincerity toward the faith during a lifetime.

➤ The law of *karma* taught that one's social position in this life was a sign of good or bad deeds performed in a previous life.

➤ There were five major levels of human castes; one moved into a higher caste because one had demonstrated good *karma* in a previous life; if a person was born into a lower caste (the lowest being the Untouchables), that soul had channeled bad *karma* through selfish deeds.

3. Throughout the centuries, the strongest social glue in South Asia was Hinduism. Empires came and went, invaders swept through the region, and other religions had some influence

on the culture, but the caste system and the elaborate Hindu traditions remained firm.

B. New belief systems arose out of Hinduism and the Hebrew religion (also known as Judaism).

1. Buddhism

    i.   Began in South Asia around 500 BCE

    ii. Founded by Prince Siddhartha Gautama (the Buddha or Enlightened One)

    iii. Maintained Hinduism's belief in reincarnation but taught that, spiritually, there was no caste system:

        ➤ Male and female, rich and poor shared the same ability to reach *nirvana*, the state of perfect oneness with the great spirit of the universe.

        ➤ The closer one was to *nirvana*, the less troubled one would be by the cares of this world. Buddhism did support the existence of social castes as a temporary, worldly condition.

    iv. The main teachings of the Buddha are found in the Four Noble Truths and the Eight-Fold Path. The Buddha maintained that the point to life and to achieving *nirvana* was to bring about the end of suffering.

        ➤ The Four Noble Truths taught:

          — In life, there is suffering.

          — Suffering comes from selfish desire.

          — Those seeking the path to *nirvana* should strive to end suffering.

          — This can be done by following the Eight-Fold Path:

            • Right View

            • Right Intention

            • Right Speech

            • Right Action

C. 600 BCE – C. 600 CE

- Right Livelihood
- Right Effort
- Right Mindfulness
- Right Concentration

    v.   The Buddha taught that questions about the existence of God were immaterial. Those who truly followed the Eight-Fold Path would find out whether there was a Supreme Being when they reached *nirvana*.

2. Christianity

    i.   Developed out of the Hebrew faith in southwest Asia during the first century CE.

    ii.   Christianity was introduced to the Hebrews in Roman-controlled Palestine by Jesus, who preached salvation through faith in him as the Son of God.

    iii.   Jesus' teachings were recorded in the Gospels and developed in other writings, particularly by his disciple Paul.

3. A similarity between Buddhism and Christianity is that both faiths taught the spiritual equality of all believers.

4. A significant difference between Buddhism and Christianity is that the Buddha himself did not promise eternal life to his followers, while Jesus did.

C. Both Buddhism and Christianity gained more followers outside their places of origin.

1. Buddhism spread east across the Indian Ocean by missionaries and merchants, and via the Silk Roads into China. Its message of peace, regardless of current circumstances, had great appeal.

    i.   The Mauryan Emperor Ashoka was an early supporter of Buddhist missionary activity.

    ii.   As Buddhism spread into East and Southeast Asia, it changed over time into a salvationist faith that saw the Buddha as a deliverer of eternal life.

     iii. This form became and remains the more popular version of Buddhism: Mahayana.

     iv. Theravada Buddhism is closer to the original form developed by the Buddha and is practiced today in Sri Lanka and parts of Southeast Asia.

  2. Christianity was initially seen by the Roman government as a religion disloyal to the emperor, and Christians were persecuted.

     i. By the fourth century CE, however, Christianity was officially accepted by Emperor Constantine.

     ii. Like Buddhism, Christianity spread by the work of missionaries and merchants, and carried west from its origins in modern-day Israel into North Africa and northwest into Turkey and Europe. Among Christianity's appeals was its promise of eternal life through faith in Jesus.

     iii. As the Roman Empire began to lose power in the West, Christianity's focus on an ever-faithful God and never-ending heavenly reward for its followers was comforting to increasing numbers of people. It remains the dominant religion in Europe.

Test Tip

The writers of the AP World History exam love to ask questions about the importance of trade routes in the spread of religions.

D. Confucius

  1. Beginning around 500 BCE, when China was undergoing great political turmoil during the Warring States period, the teachings of Confucius became the bedrock of that society.

     i. The sayings of Confucius were written after his death in *The Analects*. Confucius set out a clear set of rules for moral behavior and for family and political order.

       ➤ Filial piety—utmost respect for parents—and obedience to those in political control were two of

c. 600 BCE – c. 600 CE

his most important teachings: "Let the ruler rule as he should and the minister be a minister as he should. Let the father act as the father should and the son act as the son should."

➤ This kind of strict moral clarity shaped family and gender relations, political governance, and attitudes toward other civilizations for centuries and is still strong today.

➤ Patriarchy, the superior place of men over women in society, was firmly established in East Asian cultures by Confucius's teachings.

2. Though dynasties rose and fell over the centuries, Confucius's teachings remained strong and held society together.

Test Tip

Note that Confucius did not promise an eternal reward for following his instructions. His teachings were a philosophy for this life, not a religion. However, by the year 1200 CE, in many areas of East and Southeast Asia, Confucianism developed into a religion known as Neo-Confucianism.

E. Daoism

1. Developed in East Asia about the same time as Confucianism and was another major influence on Chinese culture.

   i. Daoism taught that there were close connections between humans and nature, a balance and harmony in all things; it also stressed deep respect for ancestors.

   ii. Whereas Confucius emphasized order in human relations, Daoism encouraged people to look away from human creations and instead find peace and balance in nature's examples.

   iii. This attention to attaining a proper balance in life influenced Chinese medical practices, such as acupuncture.

   iv. Daoist-influenced architecture sought to blend the building style into the local landscape. Examples of this blending are the famous sloping roofs that top many temples in East Asia.

2. Laozi was the best-known Daoist philosopher. The most well-known symbol of Daoism is the *Yin-Yang*. Neo-Confucianism, which incorporated some of the ideas from Buddhism and Daoism, will be discussed in Chapter 8.

Test Tip

Expect questions on the AP World History exam that compare and contrast the tenets of major world belief systems.

↳ principle or belief

F. Animism and Shamanism

1. The faiths discussed above had written guidelines to shape their followers' beliefs, but outside the core classical civilizations, animism and shamanism remained popular belief systems.

   i. *Animism* is the belief that the natural world itself has spiritual powers.

   ii. *Shamanism* is the belief that human spirit guides (shamans) are contacts between this world and the spirit world. Shamans are also believed to have the power to heal physical and spiritual illnesses.

2. Both systems held great reverence for deceased ancestors, who were thought to continue to guide the lives of the living. Areas where animism and shamanism continued to be popular in this era were Africa, the Andean region, and some parts of East Asia.

G. Belief systems and gender roles

1. Belief systems also played a major part in gender roles.

   i. While men dominated the leadership of all major religions, women often served in similar capacities as priestesses, prophets, and missionaries.

   ii. Both Buddhism and Christianity offered religious community to women by allowing them to serve as nuns.

C. 600 BCE – C. 600 CE

II. **Classical Cultures**

A. Classical civilizations and the arts

1. Classical civilizations developed many long-lasting forms of the arts, including architecture, literature, paintings, and sculptures.

   i.   Greek plays and histories influenced literature around the Mediterranean region and eventually throughout Western civilization.

   ➤ The Greeks invented theatrical acting—initially dramas with moral themes and later comedies that reflected the human condition.

   ➤ Greek histories of their wars with the Persians and among themselves became the template for Western historical writing.

   ➤ The point of history, according to the Greeks, was to teach life lessons about the consequences of good and bad behavior and decision-making. In this way, people learn to become good citizens.

   ii. Indian epic poems (among the most important are the *Ramayana* and the *Bhagavad Gita*) continue to influence literature in South Asia today with their stories of self-sacrifice and devotion to duty and to the Hindu faith.

   iii. Architecture that developed in China, India, Mesoamerica, and the Mediterranean region in the classical era had a long-lasting influence on building styles.

   ➤ In all these regions, monumental building projects supported both the government and religious faith.

   ➤ Mesoamerican temples looked very similar to Mesopotamian ziggurats from a much earlier age.

   ➤ Greek and Indian architectural styles blended as a result of Hellenism after Alexander the Great's empire reached into South Asia.

iv. In art and sculpture, religious themes prevailed in all regions.

➤ As with architecture, Greek forms of sculpture blended with North African, South Asian, and East Asian themes to be known as *Hellenistic* in style.

➤ Many sculptures throughout South and East Asia venerated Hindu, Buddhist, or Confucian beliefs.

➤ Daoist artists painted beautiful scenes of nature as part of their expression of faith.

C. 600 BCE – C. 600 CE

Chart of World Faiths*

	Hinduism	Buddhism	Daoism
Place and Time of Origin	South Asia, c. 2000 BCE	South Asia, c. 500 BCE	East Asia, c. 500 BCE
Global Reach	Primarily South Asia	East and Southeast Asia	East Asia
Founder	No single founder	Siddhartha Gautama (The Buddha)	Laozi
Principal Deity/ Dieties	Brahma, Vishnu, Shiva	Not applicable	Dao, "the way of nature"
Sacred Writings	Vedas, Upanishads, Puranas	Pali Canon, *Mahayana Sutra*	Daodejing
Principal Beliefs	Oneness with universe attained through reincarnation.	Four Noble Truths, Eight-Fold Path. Reincarnation.	Harmony found in the way of nature.
Symbol			

*You will learn about Neo-Confucianism and Islam in later chapters.

Neo-Confucianism	Judaism	Christianity	Islam
East Asia, c. 1100 CE	Southwest Asia, c. 1600 BCE	Southwest Asia, c. 35 CE	Southwest Asia, c. 630 CE
East Asia	Southwest Asia, Europe, the United States	Americas, Europe, and Oceania	North Africa and South and Southeast Asia
Han Yu, Zhu Xi	Abraham	Jesus	Muhammad
Confucius	God (Yahweh)	God	God (Allah)
Four Books	Hebrew Scriptures, including the *Torah*	New Testament	Qur'an
Respect for authority and family structure leads to salvation.	One all-powerful God. History unfolds as God's plan.	Salvation through faith in God's son Jesus	Muhammad is Allah's last prophet. Judgment for unbelievers.

c. 600 BCE – c. 600 CE

Development of City-States and Empires
c. 600 BCE–c. 600 CE

I. **The Classical Era**

In the Classical Era (c. 600 BCE–c. 600 CE), empires and city-states developed and expanded throughout Afro-Eurasia and the Americas. In the list below, pay attention to the empires and city-states in Afro-Eurasia that existed at the same time. They knew about each other and indirectly exchanged goods, technology, and ideas, and if they were near enough to each other, they often went to war.

In general, an empire had one king with political control over a large amount of territory, usually including people with a variety of cultures. Leadership did not have to be from the same family over time. Dynasties, such as those in China, are empires whose leadership flows through one family line. Sometimes dynasties in China lasted hundreds of years. City-states were powerful cities that expanded their influence over pockets of colonies. The Phoenician and Greek city-states colonized areas both near and far from their homes. Below is a list of civilizations from the Classical Era. Use it to keep in mind those civilizations that existed at the same time.

A. Must-Know Empires and City-States in the Classical Era:

1. Southwest Asia

   i.   Persian (Achaemenid) Empire (c. 550 BCE–c. 330 BCE)

   ii. Parthian Empire (c. 250 BCE–c. 220 CE)

2. East Asia

   i.   Qin Dynasty (c. 220 BCE–c. 206 BCE)

   ii. Han Dynasty (c. 206 BCE–c. 220 CE)

3. South Asia

   i.   Mauryan Empire (c. 321 BCE–c. 185 BCE)

   ii. Gupta Empire (c. 320 CE–c. 550 CE)

4. Mediterranean

   i.   Phoenician city-states and their colonies around the Mediterranean (c.1000–c. 200 BCE)

   ii. Greek city-states and their colonies around the Mediterranean (c. 600 BCE–c. 330 BCE)

   iii. Alexander's Hellenistic empires (c. 330 BCE–c. 30 BCE)

   iv. Roman Republic (c. 500 BCE–c. 30 BCE)

   v. Roman Empire (c. 30 BCE–476 CE)

   vi. Byzantine Empire (476 CE–1453 CE)

5. Mesoamerica

   i.   Teotihuacán city-state (c.100 CE–700 CE)

   ii. Mayan city-states (c. 250 CE–c. 900 CE)

6. Andean South America

   i.   Moche Empire (c. 100–c. 800 CE)

7. North America

   i. From Chaco to Cahokia

Some "must-know" empires are more "must-know" than others. Those in East Asia, the Mediterranean, and South Asia get the most attention on the exam.

II. Political Control and Contributions

A. Classical Era Empires

Classical Era empires created complex forms of governments and elaborate bureaucracies.

1. Kings had a great deal of administrative support: vice-kings ruled large portions of the empire; governors oversaw smaller territories within the empire; and city leaders reported to the governors.

2. Empires also had government record-keepers, post office officials, tax collectors, soldiers, census takers, and judges.

3. Many governments in later eras modeled their systems on these from the Classical Era.

B. The Persian Empires

The Persian empires of the Classical Era—the Achaemenid and the Parthian—are noteworthy because of their size and organization and their contacts with neighboring civilizations like the Hebrews, Phoenicians, Greeks, and Romans.

1. The first great Persian Empire (also referred to as the Achaemenid Empire) was centered in modern Iran and was the larger of the two discussed here. It stretched from Western India across modern Turkey almost to Greece.

2. The Persian Empire was so large that the king used regional leaders known as *satraps* to watch over portions of the empire and report back to him.

3. The Persians had one of the world's first highway systems. It was used by the empire's armies to move rapidly from place to place and by the king's messengers.

   i. These messengers delivered his dispatches so efficiently that admiring Greek historians marveled that "neither snow, nor rain, nor gloom of night" could keep these messengers from the swift completion of their appointed tasks.

4. In a pattern that was repeated over many centuries and in many regions around the world, the Persian Empire overextended itself and became vulnerable to attack from the outside.

   i. In the early 300s BCE, the Greek ruler Alexander the Great spent eleven years in a quest to conquer the Achaemenid Empire. He achieved his goal and this

Alexander the Great conquered Achaemenid

Persian Empire rapidly declined, but Alexander himself died soon afterward. His short-lived empire was divided among his generals.

5. After about a century, a new Persian-based empire arose—the Parthian Empire—and it defeated what still remained of Alexander's divided kingdom. The Parthians' biggest rival to the west was a new Mediterranean power based in Rome, with whom they had many clashes.

C. Chinese Dynasties

The Chinese dynasties—the Qin and the Han—are noteworthy for their religious toleration, technological achievements, and governmental system, the latter of which lasted for over 2000 years.

1. After the chaos of the Warring States period (c. 500 BCE–c. 220 BCE), the Qin Dynasty arose in East Asia.

   i. The Chinese believed that the heavens would provide them with a ruler who would establish a family line, a dynasty that would rule until its leaders displeased the powers in heaven. This mandate of heaven, like Confucianism, was an integral part of Chinese culture for centuries.

   ii. Emperor Qin Shihuangdi ("Chin Shehwungdee") returned China to dynastic rule with both diplomatic skill and military ruthlessness.

   iii. Qin Shihuangdi used a Chinese political philosophy called *legalism*, which established a clear chain of command and even clearer rules of bureaucratic etiquette. It included severe punishment for those who purposefully—or accidentally—broke those rules.

   iv. Although the Qin Dynasty didn't last very long (c. 220–206 BCE), it created a solid foundation for dynastic rule in China that endured into the early twentieth century. Other empires around the globe during the Classical Era had large, organized governmental bureaucracies—the Roman Empire, for example—but none matched the complexity of those established by the dynasties in East Asia at this time.

2. The Han Dynasty (206 BCE–220 CE) lasted much longer than the Qin Dynasty.

   i. The Han Dynasty existed at about the same time as the Roman Empire and exchanged trade and diplomatic ties with them along the Silk Roads.

   ii. The empire was roughly as large as Rome's, at least as wealthy, and certainly more technologically developed. Its capital was Chang'an (modern-day Xi'an).

   iii. Like all Classical empires, the Han Dynasty extended its power through a mix of diplomacy, trade, and military power.

   iv. The Han began building the Great Wall of China, a project that continued on and off for over 1000 years. The Great Wall was built to keep northern invaders out of the empire.

   v. The Han also began canal-digging projects that linked northern and southern China.

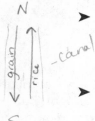

   ➤ These government-sponsored canal projects were designed to help trade. The canals allowed grain from the north to be transported to the south, and rice from the south was brought to the north.

   ➤ The canals also helped the movement of people. The Chinese government moved many people from northern areas into the south largely to promote unification under a common culture.

D. South Asia

In South Asia, the usual political situation was *not* having an empire. Instead, local and regional governance was the norm. Two important exceptions are the Mauryan and Gupta Empires.

1. The Mauryan Empire arose first (c. 321–c. 185 BCE) and stretched from modern Pakistan almost to the southern end of modern India.

   i. The most famous ruler of the Mauryan Empire was Ashoka, who converted to a peaceful life under Buddhism after years of empire-building through bloody conquest. After his conversion, he promoted the spread of Buddhism by sending Buddhist missionaries into East and Southeast Asia.

ii. Ashoka ruled in a manner that was considered almost kindly by the day's standards. Despite his efforts, however, Hinduism remained (and remains) the dominant religion in most of South Asia.

2. The Gupta Empire (c. 320 CE–c. 550 CE) covered roughly the northern half of today's India and is most notable for its cultural contributions that later found their way into Western culture.

i. The Gupta contributed the concept of zero; an efficient numbering system (later introduced to the West as "Arabic numerals"); chess; and medical advances.

Test Tip

The AP World History exam questions usually combine the Mauryan and Gupta Empires and refer to them as "Classical Indian Empires."

E. The Mediterranean

In the Mediterranean, the Phoenician city-states' contributions included an alphabet and reading from left to right. Both of these contributions eventually found their way to much of the world.

1. The Phoenicians began spreading their influence from their original base on the eastern shores of the Mediterranean, in modern-day Lebanon.

i. Using their great seafaring skills, they established colonies across the Mediterranean in Greece, Italy, North Africa, and Spain.

ii. The Phoenicians did not often use military conquest to gain power. Instead, they were interested in trade—they found out what a potential trader wanted and, more important, they knew how to get it for him or her.

iii. The Phoenicians specialized in luxury goods. In fact, words such as *diamond*, *cinnamon*, and *rose* can all trace their origins to the Phoenicians.

2. The Phoenicians' colonies in Greece greatly influenced the development of Greek civilization.

i. The Phoenician alphabet and coinage were adopted by the Greeks.

ii. The Greeks later influenced the development of the Romans.

iii. Bringing it full circle, in the third and second centuries BCE, the Romans fought one of the last great Phoenician colonies—Carthage—for economic and political control of the western Mediterranean. Rome's victory led to the rise of the Roman Republic's power in the Mediterranean region.

F. Greek City-States

The Greek city-states (c. 600 BCE–c. 330 BCE) contributed to our idea of citizen and democracy. Greek democracy, in its time, was remarkable. Even though only free adult men could be citizens and vote on government policies, the idea that government could be influenced by the peaceful voice of its people was quite unique.

1. The Greek city-states shared a common language and religion, but democracy was *not* the only form of government in all Greek city-states.

i. For example, the city-state of Athens allowed participation by its male citizenry, but Sparta was a totalitarian oligarchy, meaning that a few men made all the governmental decisions and no dissent was permitted.

ii. Political forms in other city-states in Greece usually existed somewhere between Athens and Sparta, and there were many kingdoms as well.

2. Alexander the Great united the multiple Greek city-states for the first time in their history. He then promptly led an

army to the east to conquer the rival Persian (Achaemenid) Empire in the 300s BCE.

i. After a long campaign, he conquered the Persians and expanded its borders to include Egypt and the Indus River region. Soon afterward he died. His empire was then divided up among his top generals into roughly Egypt, Southwest Asia, and Greece.

ii. The greatest legacy from Alexander the Great's conquest was Hellenism, also known as the Hellenistic culture. This was a blending of Greek math, science, philosophy, literature, governance, architecture, and art with existing forms in Egypt, which at the time included Southwest, Central, and South Asia.

> *The blending of the Greek and Egyptian cultures (Hellenism) brings up an important AP World History term—cultural syncretism. Examples include: statues of the Buddha found in South Asia with distinctive Greek styles that portray the human figure realistically; coins minted throughout the region that had Alexander's face on them; and Egyptian scientists, educated in Greek schools in Alexandria, who accurately estimated the circumference of the Earth in the second century BCE. Be sure you're familiar with this term for the AP World History exam.*

G. Roman Civilization

The Roman civilization patterned much of it politics and culture after the Greeks. Over time, the Romans passed those patterns to civilizations in Europe, Southwest Asia, and North Africa.

1. It has been said that "Rome captured Greece, but Greece captivated Rome."

   i. This quote means that the Roman army conquered Greece a century or so after Alexander's death, but then the Romans adopted many aspects of Greek culture, including architecture, philosophy, and literature.

   ii. The Romans traded in many of their gods in favor of Greek gods, but then gave them Roman names. One exception was Apollo, the god of light and poetry, whom the Romans greatly admired.

2. The Roman Classical Era includes both the Republic (c. 500 BCE–c. 30 BCE) and the Empire (c. 30 BCE–476 CE). The death of Julius Caesar and the rise of emperor Augustus marked the switch from the Roman Republic to the Roman Empire.

Test Tip

Remember: If the question on the essay portion of the AP World History exam asks for methods used for political control by the Roman Empire, you won't get credit for writing about the Republic or Julius Caesar.

3. Roman civilization was dedicated to building.

   i. The Romans built monuments as well as aqueducts that carried water over long distances into major cities. They also built roads that crossed the empire and led travelers all around the Mediterranean, into Eastern and Western Europe, and into much of Britain.

   ii. Roman roads were used by the military to move soldiers quickly into trouble spots around the empire, by merchants and travelers, and also by missionaries after the arrival of Christianity.

4. The Roman government used its military, both land and sea forces, to protect trade routes within its borders.

   i. The Romans built military fortresses throughout their empire to protect their political and economic interests. The military fought rivals around its borders over the course of hundreds of years.

   ii. The Roman military also fought people within the empire who didn't necessarily like being under Roman rule. Uprisings in Britain, Gaul (France), Germania (Germany), and Palestine (by Jewish nationalists) kept the Roman legions busy.

5. The Romans also extended their influence by using diplomats and merchants who traveled far beyond Rome's borders to broker treaties and exchange trade goods. For

c. 600 BCE–C. 600 CE

example, silk transported via the famous Silk Roads from China could be purchased by wealthy people in the city of Rome.

6. Similar to a policy enacted by the Han rulers, the Roman Republic and Empire promoted migration of many people into its colonies to encourage the spread of the "Roman way." This policy was so successful that many people from western Europe all the way into Southwest Asia were known as Roman citizens, even though they never set foot in Italy or the city of Rome.

7. Even though the western half of the Roman Empire fell in 476 CE and the city of Rome spiraled into decay, the eastern half of the empire continued on for another thousand years.

    i. Headquartered in Constantinople (Istanbul in today's Turkey), the Byzantine Empire maintained the "glory of Rome" over the eastern Mediterranean until the mid-fifteenth century CE.

    ii. The Byzantine Empire influenced the social, political, and economic development of Russia, Eastern Europe, and modern-day Turkey.

    iii. The Byzantine Empire's greatest legal contribution was its legal system, known as the *Code of Justinian*.

Test Tip

The writers of the AP World History exam love to compare the political methods and social features of the Han and Roman empires, so pay attention to those connections.

H. Mesoamerica and Andean Civilizations

The Mesoamerican (c. 100 CE–c. 900 CE) and Andean civilizations (c. 100 CE–c. 800 CE) of the Classical Era developed, of course, away from those in Afro-Eurasia. In Mesoamerica—modern southern Mexico and Central America—the city-states of the Mayan civilization and of Teotihuacán flourished near each other. The Andean people lived in northwest modern South America in the Andes Mountains.

1. The Maya made complex mathematical calculations, studied the stars, and developed a writing system. Having a writing system was one of the features of the Maya that made them stand out in the Americas. They carved words in stone and on deer hides and recorded astronomical observations, history, and religious beliefs.

2. The Maya built tall religious temples that looked like Mesopotamia's ziggurats.

3. The biggest Mayan city was Tikal, with about 50,000 people in the city and another 50,000 living nearby. Like the Egyptians, the Maya built large pyramids and temples.

   i.   The Maya also built an astronomical observatory and palaces for their royalty.

4. The Mayan agricultural system featured irrigation and terracing of hillsides and was very successful, supporting a population of about 5 million people within the empire.

5. Like all other classical civilizations, the Maya maintained power through military coercion, a tribute system of goods and people from those who were conquered, and connecting to and influencing regional trade networks.

   i.   As in other classical civilizations, there was also a close relationship between political and spiritual leaders.

   ii. Human sacrifice was an important aspect of Mayan religion.

6. Teotihuacán was a city-state located to the north of the Maya. It had a population of perhaps 200,000 people—making it one of the biggest cities in the world in the Classical Era.

   i.   Teotihuacán was a separate civilization from the Maya and had a complex government bureaucracy, reservoirs, apartment complexes made of stone, and (like the Maya) pyramids dedicated to their gods.

   ii. The Mayan and Teotihuacán civilizations traded with each other and, at times, waged war against each other.

C. 600 BCE–C. 600 CE

7. The Moche was the classical civilization of the Andean region (c. 100–c. 800 CE).

   i.   The Moche inhabited territory that stretched about 250 miles along the mountains of the western coast of modern Peru.

   ii. The Moche government was controlled by a class of warrior-priests.

   iii. Much like the Maya, the Moche built pyramids and other monumental buildings, such as palaces. They traded with neighbors, created complex irrigation systems, terraced mountainsides to grow crops, and practiced human sacrifice.

   iv. Moche craftspeople created some of the world's most beautiful works of art in gold, jewels, and pottery.

The Mesoamerican and Andean civilizations receive little attention on the AP World History exam compared to those in Eurasia because most Global History classes in colleges don't spend much time on them. Note, however, that the AP World History curriculum calls the Maya, the Teotihuacán, and the Moche "must-know" civilizations, so be prepared.

III. Common Features of Classical Empires and City-States

In this chapter, similarities between the classical civilizations in the Americas and in Afro-Eurasia have been noted. Below is a summary of those similarities.

A. Cities were important parts of all empires and, of course, among city-states. They were centers of trade, art, and religious and governmental buildings.

   1. The Mediterranean civilizations

      i. Alexandria and the city-state of Carthage in North Africa

      ii. Rome in Italy

  iii. Constantinople between the Black Sea and the Mediterranean in Asia Minor

  iv. The city-state of Athens in Greece

 2. East Asia

  i. Chang'an, capital of the Han Dynasty in China

 3. Mesoamerica

  i. The city-state of Teotihuacán

Test Tip

> For the AP World History exam, be sure you know some important cities of the Classical Era and be able to locate them on a map.

B. Social structures were quite similar among all classical empires, with political and religious elites at the top, followed by (in varying order of status depending on the civilization) merchants, warriors, craftspeople, laborers, and slaves.

 1. Slaves were at the bottom of all societies. The Mayans and Romans were much more dependent on slave labor than the Han in East Asia.

 2. The East Asian dynasties [China] were the only ones to consider merchants to be near the bottom of the social ladder. Merchants were thought to be of little value because they exchanged goods, but produced nothing by their own hands.

 3. In the Mauryan and Gupta Empires of South Asia, one's social status was predetermined by the caste one was born into, and there was nothing in this life that could change that.

C. Agricultural and other labor was provided by free people, indentured servants, and slaves in the classical societies.

 1. Often, people were forced to provide free labor (*corvée*) to the government in road-building and other projects.

2. Two examples of government-required labor were the hundreds of thousands of peasants who were mandated to participate in the construction of the Great Wall and the Grand Canal in China.

D. A continuity through time was certainly evident during the Classical Era. Patriarchy—male domination of political, social, and economic life—was common to all the classical empires.

 IV. The Decline and Fall of the Classical Empires

A. All of the classical empires eventually overextended themselves, declined in political, social, and economic areas, and ultimately fell. This happened at different times but usually along the same pattern: internal disruptions and outside invasions led to the demise of each.

1. In Afro-Eurasia, the Mauryan, Han, Western Roman, and Gupta Empires collapsed, in that order. The usual chain of events included a long but serious decline in political, social, and economic influence over its own people and then those outside the empire's borders.

2. Internal pressures included:

   i. Diseases spread by war and by transference along trade routes

   ii. Peasant revolts against overbearing landlords

   iii. Resistance to high taxation

   iv. A breakdown of imperial authority

   v. Failing economies

3. One example of an internal rebellion came within the Han Dynasty with the Yellow Turban revolt, which promised a new society with no rich landlords and no oppressive government officials to bully the peasants into labor projects.

4. External pressures came from rival empires, local rebels, and nomadic groups who took advantage of thinning numbers of the hated empire's military as it began to decline.

   i.   Nomadic invaders (barbarians) swept through farms and cities of all the classical empires, looting and taking food, and leaving destruction and death behind.

   ii. The most famous barbarian invaders of Rome were the Huns, Goths, and Vandals, who attacked the Western Roman Empire and the capital of Rome itself in the mid-fifth century CE.

B. Not every classical empire fell in the same manner.

1. The Han Dynasty's demise, for example, fell largely because of internal causes, including struggles for power among the dynastic family members and top generals, as well as the Yellow Turban revolt.

2. The causes of decline and fall of the classical empires in the Americas remain a mystery and a source of debate among historians.

   i.   Current theories point to ecological collapse, perhaps brought on by overuse of the land or perhaps by natural changes in the climate. Either theory would have lead to lower levels of food production.

   ii. Without abundant and dependable sources of food, residents of cities such as Teotihuacán, Tikal, and those in the Moche Empire perished.

Development of Communication and Trade Networks

c. 600 BCE – c. 600 CE

The development of the classical empires led to increased connections between people, even for those separated by thousands of miles. The majority of these connections occurred because of trade: luxury items or raw materials were exchanged for money or other goods. Other connections that developed involved the transfer of technologies and religions between regions. One important unintended consequence of these exchanges along trade routes was the spread of diseases, which killed millions of people across Afro–Eurasia.

Technology and faith usually piggybacked the goods that merchants carried across Afro-Eurasia by land and by sea. In contrast, in the Americas during the Classical Era, the amount and complexity of trade and the distances covered by merchants were not nearly as well developed.

Test Tip

Trade is one of the most important and recurring themes in AP World History. You'll definitely see questions (and possibly essays) that ask about trade.

I. The Land Networks of Africa, Europe, and Asia

A. Geography

Geography determined what was exchanged, where it was exchanged, and by whom it was exchanged.

1. Climate and topography (mountains, plains, deserts, rivers, seas)

     i.   Climate and topography determine where valuable minerals are found, the types of plants that can be grown, and where seaports, mountain passes, and oases exist so that raw materials may be processed and sold;

     ii.   Merchants needed to transport these goods with relative safety across regions.

2. Trade happens because people want goods.

     i.   For example, salt has always been an important trade good, used not so much to flavor food as it is used today, but rather to preserve food in the millennia before refrigeration. People went to great lengths (literally) to get it—some traveled from Southwest Asia or Central Africa across the Sahara Desert to Northwest Africa to get salt.

     ii.   Merchants were willing to make difficult treks in hopes of receiving a nice payoff for their efforts.

     iii.   Visualize the Afro-Eurasia trade network as a web—which allowed wealthy Romans to buy silk clothing that was made in China; merchants transported silk and other goods for a couple of hundred miles and handed the goods off to the next merchant caravan, got money for their part of the trip, and headed back home for more.

     iv.   The silk (or tea, or spices, or salt) was relayed from town to town until it reached its final destination.

B. The Silk Roads

1. The most extensive of the land-based trade routes in the world at this time were the Silk Roads, named because of the highly valued silk that was traded.

     i.   For centuries, only China knew how to make silk—a light, soft, and durable fabric. These qualities made silk highly desirable and expensive, so only wealthy elites could afford it.

2. Other items traded along the Silk Roads:

    i.   From East Asia to points west: horses, spices, furs, ivory, perfumes, lacquered boxes and furniture, rice, wool, tea, and porcelain (you know, "china")

    ii.   From South Asia to points east and west: cotton, spices, sandalwood, rice

    iii. From Central Asia to points east, west, and south: dates, almonds, fruit, camels, horses

    iv. From points west (the Black Sea and Mediterranean regions) to the east and south: glass, gold, furs, amber, cattle, olive oil, perfumes

3. The exchange of grains and fabrics across Eurasia changed farming techniques and allowed crops to grow in new regions.

    i.   The *qanat system*, a form of irrigation, transports water from below ground to the surface in arid regions.

    ii.   Knowledge and use of the qanat system from Central Asia spread into other regions, particularly Southwest Asia.

4. Merchants and missionaries from South Asia introduced Buddhism along the Silk Roads, which had long-lasting effects on East and Southeast Asia.

    i.   When the Han Empire began to decline, many people in China converted to Buddhism.

5. Disease was also transported along the Silk Roads.

    i.   Pandemic (widespread) diseases such as the bubonic plague (the Black Death) frequently crossed Afro-Eurasia along trade routes.

    ii.   The devastating effects of these diseases are thought to be one of the reasons for the fall of the Han Dynasty.

6. Tea and horse caravan roads extended from southern China to South Asia.

    i.   Though not as well known as the Silk Roads, they were vital exchange routes.

C. 600 BCE – C. 600 CE

Test Tip — *The effects of trade and the items traded along the Silk Roads are important topics on the AP World History exam.*

C. Sahara Caravan Routes

1. Commerce across North Africa

   i. Along the Mediterranean coast were coastal cities and ports, rich in vegetation and resources.

   ii. Commodities like dates, cotton, dyes, cloth, leather goods, and glass were supplied from these cities and ports.

   iii. South of the "rim" of Mediterranean Africa is the Sahara Desert. Merchants who ventured into it exchanged those items and carried out gold, salt, ivory, animal hides, and slaves, connecting into the Silk Road network.

2. Introduction of the camel

   i. In North Africa around the turn of the calendar from BCE to CE, the camel was introduced as a means of transporting goods. This led to a major increase in the amount of trade that occurred between West Africa and Southwest Asia.

   ii. In the next era, c. 600–c. 1450, Islam was carried into the Trans-Saharan region along trade routes, just as Buddhism had spread into East Asia earlier.

D. North-South Eurasian Routes

1. The Silk Roads ran roughly east to west. Directly connected to the Silk Roads were more networks of trade routes that run north and south, and linked Central Asia to South and Southwest Asia.

   i. Along these trade routes, merchants carried merchandise such as cotton, spices, and rice from South Asia; spices from Southeast Asia; and horses and textiles (cloth) to and from Central Asia.

    ii.   These routes also connected to the edges of the Baltic Sea in Europe, involving Russia and the Black Sea trade connections.

    iii. Constantinople, the capital of the Byzantine Empire, was a key center that linked these exchange routes together.

II. **The Sea Networks of Africa, Europe, and Asia Developed Extensive Trade Networks by Sea**

A. The Indian Ocean Trading Network

    1. The Indian Ocean trading network was the largest sea trading area in the world until Europeans began crossing the Atlantic in the late 1400s.

        i.   The Indian Ocean connected Southeast Asia and China to Africa, the Middle East, and South Asia.

        ii. It was a major conveyor of Buddhism from South Asia into East and Southeast Asia, and in the next era, c. 600–c. 1450, Muslim merchants and missionaries carried their faith from the Middle East across the Indian Ocean into the same regions.

        iii. Many of the items that were carried along the Silk Roads and the other Eurasian land routes were also exchanged across the Indian Ocean: silk, cotton, rice, spices, horses, ivory, gold, porcelain, and people.

    2. All sea trade depended on ocean currents and wind, and this is true of the Indian Ocean.

        i.   The monsoon winds blow along the East African coast toward South Asia in the summer and down the East African coast in the winter. This natural "clock" helped merchants plan the timing and content of their shipments.

        ii. Small but seaworthy trading ships used by Arab merchants, called *dhows*, used a triangular lateen sail to follow these winds.

C. 600 BCE – C. 600 CE

    iii. Arab shipbuilding and navigation skills spread quickly along the sea trade routes.

  3. People interacted via the Indian Ocean trade routes: East Asians, South Asians, East African Swahilis, Arabs from Southwest Asia, Malays from Southeast Asia, Turks, Greeks, and Russians participated.

Test Tip

In past AP World History exams, questions on the effects of trade and the items traded across the Indian Ocean have frequently been included.

B. The Mediterranean and Black Sea Trading Areas

  1. Beginning with the Egyptians and Phoenicians, and continued by the Greeks, Romans, and Byzantines, the Mediterranean Sea network of trade was vast and long-lasting.

    i. Olives, pottery, glass, woodwork, leather, and wool textiles were exchanged across all parts of the Mediterranean world.

    ii. Out of Africa, merchants traded gold, ivory, salt, copper, and slaves across and around the Mediterranean.

    iii. During the first century CE and continuing for many centuries, Christianity was carried into eastern and western Europe and Africa on foot by missionaries and merchants, but especially by boats that carried cargo and people across the Mediterranean.

  2. The Black Sea, with Asia on its eastern shore and Europe on its western coastline, was another important trading area before, during, and after the Classical Era.

    i. Constantinople (known as Byzantium in ancient times) was one of the world's great points of exchange.

    ii. Through the Black Sea, merchants carried goods from the Silk Roads, the Mediterranean, and Russia.

     iii. In the next era, c. 600–c.1450, merchants unwittingly carried the bubonic plague—the Black Death—into western Europe.

III. Exchanging Goods in the Americas

A. The Americas Exchanged Goods but on a Much Smaller Scale than in Afro-Eurasia

    1. Several factors explain the contrast in the amount of goods traded in the Americas to that of Afro-Eurasia:

       i. There were far fewer people in the Americas. Historians estimate that of the roughly 250 million people on Earth in the first century CE, only about 12 million lived in all of North and South America.

      ii. Because there were fewer types of large domesticated animals in the Americas, the wheel was never developed for transportation until the Europeans arrived in the early fifteenth century CE.

     iii. The llama and the alpaca were used as pack animals in the Andes; in other parts of the Americas, dogs pulled sleds loaded with materials.

     iv. The narrow and jungle-covered terrain of the Isthmus of Panama made trade from South America into Central and North America very difficult.

    2. Despite these demographic and geographic limitations, there is an indication of exchanges of plants, including tobacco and corn; and manufactured goods, such as pottery, jewelry (made with gold, turquoise or turtle shells); and clothing made from animal skins.

       i. These exchanges were probably made in relay fashion, from one village and city to another, and not by merchants on long-distance trade missions.

      ii. American corn (maize) was developed first in Mesoamerica and then spread to regions north and south along trade connections.

C. 600 BCE – C. 600 CE

iii. The areas in the Americas with the most trade activity were among the Maya and Teotihuacán in Mesoamerica and within the Moche civilization of the Andes.

PERIOD 3

REGIONAL AND INTERREGIONAL INTERACTIONS

c. 600 CE – c. 1450 CE

Expansion of Networks of Exchange

c. 600 CE – c. 1450 CE

The years c. 600–c. 1450 are referred to by many historians as the Post-Classical Era. The most important development during this era was the introduction and spread of Islam from its place of origin in Southwest Asia into North and Northwest Africa and East, Central, and Southeast Asia. The spread of Islam had tremendous social, political, and economic effects throughout Afro-Eurasia.

The resurrection of western Europe after the fall of the Roman Empire in 476 and the rise of the Tang and Song dynasties in China are other very important developments in this era.

The number of people and amount of goods, ideas, technology, and diseases that crossed Afro-Eurasia increased tremendously compared to the previous period. In the Americas, new empires arose, but north-south exchanges across those continents did not change much from the earlier era. Finally, migrations of people in Oceania in this time period affected the environments they entered, as well as their own cultures.

I. Technological Changes and Trading Practices

A. Cities Increased in Number and Importance

   1. Cities along land and sea trade routes increased in number and importance in this era.

      i.   Important Afro-Eurasian trading cities along land routes in this era included Djenne (also known as Jenne), Timbuktu, and Gao in West Africa; Byzantium and Novgorod in Europe; Baghdad in Southwest Asia;

Samarkand and Bukhara in Central Asia; and Dunhuang and Chang'an in East Asia.

ii. Important seaports included: Venice and Byzantium in Europe; Tyre and Hormuz in Southwest Asia; Zanzibar and Kilwa on East Africa's Swahili Coast; Calicut and Goa (not to be confused with Gao above) in South Asia; Melaka (Malacca) in Southeast Asia; and Hangzhou and Guangzhou in East Asia.

B. Luxury and Everyday Items Exchanged

1. Through these cities and trade routes, many luxury and everyday items were exchanged, and in greater quantity than ever before.

   i. Silk remained a highly prized luxury commodity throughout Afro-Eurasia.

   ii. Trade items continued to be exchanged but *new* technologies, goods, and ideas were a change in this era, including items from China such as gunpowder, paper, the compass, and the astrolabe. (The astrolabe was a device for sea navigation.)

2. Land and sea merchants carried Islam into South Asia, East Asia, and Southeast Asia from the Middle East.

Test Tip

You don't have to memorize all of the examples mentioned above, but the writers of the AP World History exam will expect you to know at least one major trade city from each region, and what items were traded through that city. Your World History textbook should show maps of these trade cities and detailed charts of the items traded.

C. New Government Policies Allowed Growth of Trade

1. With the fall of the Han Dynasty in China in the third century CE, trade along the Silk Roads and in the Indian Ocean region declined because the political unrest and instability in those regions made travel riskier.

fall of Han =
↓ in trade

i. When the Tang (618–907) and Song (960–1279) Dynasties reestablished government stability in East Asia, they provided security and actively supported trade by land and sea.

ii. Chinese land merchants crossed into Central Asia in greater than ever numbers, and sea merchants sailed into Southeast Asia, across the Indian Ocean into South Asia, East Africa, and the Middle East (which is part of Southwest Asia).

2. The greatest government decision regarding trade in the Indian Ocean region was the decision *not* to interfere.

i. Chinese emperors chose to let the Indian Ocean merchants manage their own affairs. Therefore, the Indian Ocean system of exchange was, for all intents and purposes, self-governing. Merchants made the rules, worked their best deals for access to ports, kept smugglers (pirates) at bay, and established prices.

ii. During the Ming Dynasty (1368–1644), the emperor sent expeditions of huge ships and thousands of men to the Indian Ocean region, but they did not attempt to take over the trading system.

3. Money was minted and printed by governments to facilitate trade.

i. Coins were minted as early as the era of the Persian (Achaemenid) Empire around 500 BCE and the concept spread throughout the Mediterranean region. Chinese merchants probably produced the first paper money before the ninth century CE. However, the Tang government in China took over that enterprise as a way of standardizing their monetary system. Some "paper" money in China was actually made of silk. (The Chinese called it flying money.)

ii. In the fourteenth century, the Mongols introduced paper money into Central and Southwest Asia. In Europe, paper money didn't catch on until the seventeenth century.

4. The Chinese government also aided trade by beginning the Grand Canal project during the Sui Dynasty (581–618 CE). Construction continued through the Tang and Song Dynasties and was finally completed during the Mongol (Yuan) era. (1271–1368). The Grand Canal links China's major rivers in a north-south fashion and allows goods to move more easily from the interior sections of the country to the capital. It is still one of China's most important transportation methods today.

D. Other Empires Connected to Trade

1. Along with the Chinese dynasties, other empires in Afro-Eurasia were intensely connected to trade.

   i. The Byzantine Empire was a major political, economic, and social power in the eastern half of the Mediterranean region. Its armies and navies provided protection for trade routes in the Mediterranean.

   ii. The Muslim caliphates and the Mongol empires of Southwest and Central Asia kept trade routes open through both violent and peaceful means across Dar-al Islam and during the *Pax Mongolica*, respectively.

II. How the Movement of People Was Both Caused and Affected by Environment, Language, and Religion

A. From c. 800–c. 1100 CE, the Vikings of northern Europe adapted to their harsh sea environment by developing ships tough enough to sail to and raid England, France, Russia, Italy, and the Byzantine Empire, often concentrating on ports of trade.

1. They were also known as Northmen, Norsemen, and Normans.

2. In England and France, they influenced the development of languages and were assimilated over time into mainstream European culture by accepting Christianity.

3. Christianity began to become popular in western Europe after the fall of Rome in the fifth century CE.

4. Vikings sailed to and colonized northern France (Normandy), Russia, Iceland, Greenland, and North America. They settled permanently in all of these places except North America.

B. In Southwest Asia, Muslim Arabs domesticated camels and introduced them into North Africa's Sahara trade network.

C. In Central Asia, nomads like the Mongols made horsemanship the major characteristic of their civilization. Their amazing horsemanship skills were one reason why their armies were so effective against lesser-prepared enemies across Asia.

for Mongols: horses = effective army

D. World Religions and Syncretism

1. *Syncretism* means "blending," and it is especially useful in studying major religions.

   i. Islam, Christianity, and Buddhism are popularly known as world-class religions. That is, over time, each one of them expanded into every inhabited continent. To obtain this global status, a religion had to adapt its beliefs and practices to local conditions. For example:

      ➤ Buddhism, as it emerged from India, didn't address questions about God, or gods, or eternal life, but as it spread into East and Southeast Asia, it adapted to the spiritual expectations of local traditions by becoming a salvationist faith that promised eternal life. This form, known as Mahayana Buddhism, is much more popular today than the original version, known as Theravada Buddhism.

      ➤ Christianity incorporated some Roman polytheistic beliefs by including prayers to patron saints who would intervene with God on the believer's behalf. Similarly, when Christianity spread to the Americas, it adapted local customs such as the Day of the Dead from the Aztec faith.

➤ Islam also modified its customs to fit local belief systems. For example, when Muslims encountered Hindus in South Asia, some blending of the faiths occurred, which is reflected in the mystical Sufi branch of Islam.

—An important example of Islamic syncretism is its teaching of tolerance for "The People of the Book." Jews and Christians are mentioned in the Qur'an as fellow believers in one God who should be allowed to maintain their faiths and not be obliged to convert to Islam.

—When Islam reached South Asia, however, it was determined that Hindus and Buddhists were also "People of the Book" even though they aren't specifically mentioned in the Qur'an. A practical explanation for this interpretation of the Qur'an might be that after considering the overwhelming numbers of Hindus in South Asia, Muslim religious leaders thought it wise to expand their definition of "People of the Book."

E. Another cross-cultural exchange in the era c. 600 CE–c. 1450 CE was the continuing and steady migration of Bantu-speaking peoples from Central Africa to East and Southeast Africa. As they encountered new environments and people, they used technology to alter the landscape and the societies.

1. Beginning about 1500 BCE and continuing through about 1000 CE, the people of Central Africa who spoke the Bantu-based languages migrated east and south into forested regions. They carried knowledge of agriculture, animal herding, and metal-working and used these skills to change the environments they encountered.

2. Bantu-based languages became the standard in Southern and Eastern Africa. Modern anthropologists traced languages currently used in southern and eastern Africa back to their roots with the Bantus of Central Africa. For example, Swahili, found today in East and South-Central Africa, is a Bantu-based language.

F. Like the Bantu-based languages, Latin-based Romance languages, such as French and Spanish, diffused across western Europe after the fall of the western Roman Empire.

   1. Similar to the ways religions change as they "move," languages often change over time as they spread.

   2. Another example of changes to languages as they move through time and across regions is how Arabic-based languages spread across North Africa in this era, carried by Islamic merchants.

Test Tip *The Bantu migration is a frequently seen topic on the AP World History exam.*

G. In the Pacific, since prehistoric times, people migrated from the Southeast Asian mainland to the many island groups in Oceania, including Australia, New Zealand, the Solomon Islands, and Hawaii.

   1. They carried with them their languages, religious beliefs, foods, and animals.

   2. Food and animals effected environmental changes. For example, people migrating into the Pacific islands by ocean-going outrigger canoes took coconuts and banana plants with them and grew them in their new homelands. As with their studies of the Bantu, modern anthropologists have examined the languages and oral tales of creation and other aspects of faith of the Polynesians across Oceania to trace their migration routes.

III. Cross-Cultural Interactions Intensify

A. A sign of the importance and economic value of trade in this era was that merchants from a great variety of cultures settled into areas far from their homelands and established pockets of communities.

c. 600 CE – c. 1450 CE

1. Jewish and Christian merchants and their families lived in major trade cities in China, South Asia, Central Asia, North Africa, western Europe, the Byzantine Empire, and the Persian Gulf region.

2. Muslim communities were established in trading cities around the rim of the Indian Ocean, Southeast Asia, North Africa, West Africa, Muslim Spain, the Byzantine Empire, and China.

3. Sogdian merchants from Persia traveled east and west across the Silk Roads, establishing communities from the Byzantine Empire to China. Their greatest contribution to history was their translation of religious texts, which included works from Islam, Christianity, Zoroastrianism, and Buddhism.

4. Chinese merchants established residences in Southeast Asia and, like Muslim merchants, in cities throughout the Indian Ocean region.

5. All the cultures represented in this merchant diaspora were drawn by the chance to earn money. Cooperative governments, who gained income and cross-cultural insights from these contacts, aided the merchants. For example, Chinese emperors welcomed ambassadors from foreign lands and even imported exotic animals like giraffes from Africa.

B. Famous travelers recorded tales of their journeys throughout Afro-Eurasia and provided insights into Post-Classical civilizations

1. One of the most famous of these travelers is the Christian merchant Marco Polo, who journeyed in the late thirteenth century CE with his merchant father and uncle from Venice to Southwest Asia along the Silk Roads into East Asia. He returned 24 years later via Southeast Asia and the Indian Ocean.

   i. Marco Polo's account of his travels, *A Description of the World*, gave literate Europeans insights into the regions he visited. Other Europeans had been to Central and East Asia before Polo, of course, but none had as great an effect on European society.

ii. Two hundred years later, Christopher Columbus used Polo's book as inspiration for his expedition to "the East" and referenced Polo's term for China, "Cathay," in his own journals.

2. Ibn Battuta was a Muslim traveler from North Africa who, in the early 1300s CE, began a journey that lasted 30 years throughout Dar al-Islam (meaning roughly "everywhere Islam is") across Afro-Eurasia.

   i. Battuta traveled to West Africa, Muslim Spain, North Africa, the Byzantine Empire, the Islamic Caliphates in Southwest Asia, East Africa, South Asia, Southeast Asia, and East Asia. His journals are full of lively commentary on the people, sights, and customs of each region he visited. It is estimated that Battuta traveled about 75,000 miles.

3. Other travelers during this era included Mansa Musa, the king of the wealthy West African kingdom of Mali, who journeyed to Mecca on a hajj in the fourteenth century. On the way, he passed through Timbuktu, Gao, and Cairo. It was recorded that he handed out so much gold that he caused a spike in inflation in Cairo.

C. Technology, ideas, and diseases were exchanged as cross-cultural encounters occurred.

1. The era c. 600–c.1450 was one of great exchanges of technology, almost all of which went from the eastern side of Afro-Eurasia, particularly from China through India westward, eventually filtering into Europe.

   i. From China came paper-making, printing, the compass, gunpowder, and cannons.

   ii. China was not just sending technology; it was receiving technology too. For example, from India, China learned how to grow and process cotton and sugar. From Vietnam in Southeast Asia, new types of rice that adapted well to southern China's growing conditions were introduced.

C. 600 CE – C. 1450 CE

    iii. Through the exchanges triggered by merchants, India "exported" many mathematical concepts, such as negative numbers and zero, into western Europe, first into Muslim-controlled Spain in this era.

2. Muslim scholars preserved the libraries of Greek literature and science left throughout the empire by Alexander the Great hundreds of years before.

3. Europeans rediscovered their Greek and Roman heritage through contact with Muslims in Spain.

    i. This new acquaintance with their classical past sparked the European Renaissance beginning in the fourteenth century.

4. The arts also "moved" along the Silk Roads and other trade routes.

    i. Musical instruments that westerners know as cymbals, tambourines, and the guitar had their origins in East and Central Asia.

    ii. Hindu and Buddhist sculptures and temples were constructed not just in South Asia, but also in Southeast Asia and China by marvelous craftspeople who were dedicated to their Buddhist faith.

5. Not everything that was exchanged had a positive effect on Afro-Eurasia.

    i. The bubonic plague, also known as the Black Death, killed huge numbers of people in this era.

    ii. The worst epidemic occurred in the fourteenth century CE and is often attributed to the expansion of trade under Mongol rule in East and Central Asia. From there, the Black Death entered the Black Sea region of the Byzantine Empire and continued into western Europe, carried unintentionally by merchant caravans. It is estimated that western Europe lost one-third of its population.

Origins and Diffusion Routes for Selected Religions (Christianity, Islam, Hinduism, and Buddhism)

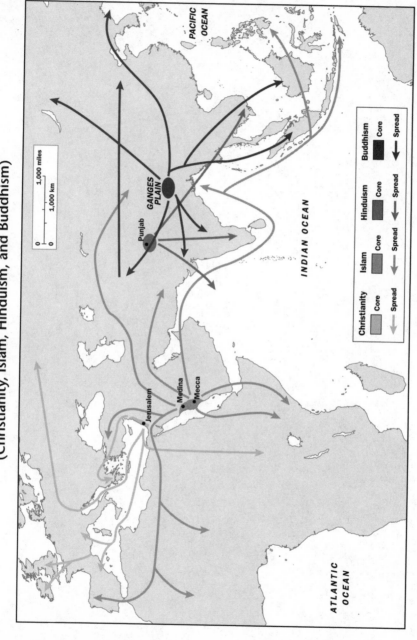

Governments in the Post-Classical Era

c. 600–c. 1450 CE

As you read in Chapter 7, the era c. 600–c. 1450 CE is often referred to as the Post-Classical Era. The Post-Classical Era saw significant civilizations rise, such as the Byzantine, Abbasid, Tang, Song, and Mongol (Yuan) empires and dynasties. Some emerged from empires that had collapsed near the end of the Classical Era; others, particularly the Muslim empires, were new governments. As in previous chapters, we will focus mainly on those in Afro-Eurasia.

I. Classical Empires Fall

A. The Roman Empire in the western Mediterranean fell in 476 CE.

   1. With the fall of the Roman Empire at the beginning of the Post-Classical Era, western Europe collapsed into an "every man for himself" situation with no unifying armies, laws, or educational systems.

      i.   The Christian church remained intact and, in the social and political vacuum left by the fall of Rome, emerged to fulfill those duties. Most western Europeans flocked to the church seeking comfort in faith, but more than that, the hierarchy in Rome also provided dearly needed social order and political stability.

     ii.   The pope served not only as the spiritual leader in western Europe, but through the organization of the Catholic Church, he was also the de facto political head of Europe.

      iii. The pope was served by bishops with regional spiritual and political authority and also by priests who served on the local level.

      iv. Change occurred as the era continued because the hierarchy expanded to include cardinals and archbishops who served as more layers of authority between the pope and bishops.

> ➤ Serving in education and missionary work were monks and nuns, men and women who lived in communities under the authority of a local priest. Note that membership in a community of nuns offered women opportunities for leadership, something almost unheard of in Europe's secular world.

2. The secular leadership that *did* exist in Western Europe at the beginning of this era was local.

      i. Land owners ("lords") ran large farms, or manors, with poor landless peoples ("serfs") working the land.

      ii. Privately hired soldiers—knights—protected their lord's land from attacks by rival lords, bandits, and sometimes Vikings.

      iii. Over time, the winners gained more land and more power until a lord had enough power to declare himself king of his country.

3. Change was on the way in western Europe as political power began to shift back into secular hands around 700 CE.

      i. It began when Charles Martel, a Christian leader of the Germanic Franks, defeated a Muslim army that had entered France from Spain in the Battle of Tours. (See below for details about Muslim Spain.)

      ii. In 800 CE, Martel's grandson, Charlemagne, united much of modern France, Germany, and northern Italy into a "New Roman Empire"—the first large secular government in western Europe since the fall of Rome.

       iii. This began a power struggle for political authority with Christian church leaders that lasted for centuries in western Europe.

  4. Charlemagne's empire fractured after his death, but this led to the formation of new types of government in western Europe—in particular, kingdoms in England and France.

       i.   Struggles between the secular rulers of these and other western European nations and Christian church leaders continued.

  5. Although the Western Roman Empire fell in 476, the Eastern Roman, or Byzantine Empire, flourished.

       i.   At its height, it was one of the most powerful empires in the world, covering eastern Europe and almost all of North Africa.

       ii. The greatest leader of the Byzantine Empire was Justinian, who, in c. 550 CE, established a unified legal code throughout his empire.

       iii. Byzantine merchants traded not only all over the Mediterranean region, but also throughout the regions surrounding the Black Sea, the Red Sea, and the Indian Ocean.

       iv. During most of its history, the Byzantine Empire was in conflict with nearby Muslim caliphates and by the end of the period was on the verge of collapse at the hands of Muslim forces.

B. Muslim empires arose in Southwest Asia, North Africa, and South Asia.

  1. Islam developed in Southwest Asia in the early seventh century CE.

       i.   Muhammad, a merchant, preached monotheism and Arab unity in a region that was mostly polytheistic and politically fragmented.

       ii. Muhammad's visions and teachings were recorded in the Qur'an.

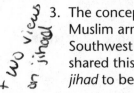

Many converted to Islam b/c it was cheaper !!

two views on jihad

2. Essential Islamic theology includes the belief in one God (Allah), that Muhammad is God's prophet, and dedication to the Five Pillars.

   i. Among other obligatory acts, the Five Pillars require that each follower of Islam (a Muslim) must take a holy journey—a *hajj*—to Mecca at least once in his lifetime, pray throughout the day, and pay a tax (*zakat*) to help the poor. Mecca was revered because it was the birthplace of Muhammad.

   ii. Note that Muhammad did not claim to be a savior, but he did preach that he was a prophet—the last and greatest of Allah's prophets.

   iii. The *zakat* (tax) was much higher for nonbelievers. This economic factor led many to convert to Islam.

3. The concept of *jihad*, or struggle for the faith, inspired Muslim armies to conquer the lands of nonbelievers in Southwest Asia and across North Africa. Not all Muslims shared this aggressive view of *jihad*. Instead, they considered *jihad* to be an inward struggle for faith.

4. Islam had an almost instant effect on the polytheistic nomadic herders of the Arabian Peninsula, uniting them into one faith, either by force or by choice.

   i. From there, Islamic armies, missionaries, and merchants rapidly spread the faith eastward and westward—so rapidly that one hundred years after Muhammad's death, Muslims and Christians fought for control of France at the Battle of Tours in 732 CE.

   ii. By that date, Islam had replaced Christianity as the dominant culture in North Africa and in Spain.

   iii. Muslim political and social influence (Dar al-Islam) stretched from Spain, across North Africa, and into modern-day India and Pakistan by the mid-eighth century CE.

5. Like Judaism and Christianity, Islam is a monotheistic faith that developed in Southwest Asia. In contrast to Christianity, where Jesus named Peter his successor, Islam did not

establish a clear line of succession after Muhammad, and the faith fractured into regional *caliphates.*

i. The *Umayyad caliphate* originally ruled from Damascus, Syria, but after clashing with the rival Abbasid caliphate (see below) it established a dynasty in Cordoba, Spain.

    ➤ Muslim rule was supreme in Spain until its peak in the eleventh century CE, and remained an important presence there until the late fifteenth century.

    ➤ While the rest of western Europe worked to recover from the collapse of the Roman Empire, Spain was wealthy and stable under the Umayyad caliphate.

    ➤ Arab technology and trade, passed down by merchants and others from Asia, kept Spain out of the discord that the rest of western Europe experienced during the Middle Ages.

ii. The *Abbasid caliphate* (c. 750–c. 1250 CE) was centered in Baghdad and stretched, at its peak in the tenth century CE, from modern Turkey into Central Asia and across North Africa. *— Very diverse!*

    ➤ *Baghdad* was one of the world's most cosmopolitan cities, with Arabs, Persians, Europeans, Turks, South Asians, Christians, Jews, Buddhists, and Muslims living there.

    ➤ The Abbasids participated in a great deal of cultural borrowing. They adapted cultural traits from neighbors and made them their own. For example, many Persians served in the government, and Persian art, language, and literature were prominent among the Abbasids, including the stories of "Aladdin" and "Sinbad the Sailor" from *1001 Nights* (*The Arabian Nights*).

    ➤ Turkish Muslims from the north, among them the Seljuks, held important posts in the Abbasid caliphate.

➤ The Abbasids also employed Turkish soldiers—*Mamluks*—in their army.

➤ Over time, the Abbasids lost power to local rulers and faced peasant revolts throughout the empire, and were ultimately destroyed by Mongols in the mid-thirteenth century.

➤ The fall of the Abbasids reflected a pattern that we read about in earlier chapters: Inner strife plus invasion from the outside led to their decline and fall.

iii. Historians often refer to the Abbasid era as the Islamic Golden Age, when scholars, poets, scientists, and artists from inside and outside the caliphate were welcomed into the region. For example, the Abbasids believed "the ink of the scholar is more holy than the blood of the martyr." Advances were made in astronomy, medicine, and mathematics (including algebra, which comes from the Arabic word "al-jabr"), just to name a few. Literature, like the above-mentioned *1001 Nights*, also included poetry and philosophy.

Test Tip

The AP World History exam pays more attention to the Abbasids than the other Muslim caliphates, but the Iberian (Spanish) caliphate is also important.

6. The political center of Islam in South Asia was at Delhi.

i. The *Delhi sultanates* were a series of Muslim Turk dynasties who settled in the northern portion of South Asia.

ii. The *Delhi sultanates* fought invaders, especially the Mongols, and sometimes blended Islam with aspects of the Hindu culture found in the region. An example is the Sikh faith.

iii. In contrast to Muslim successes converting the peoples they encountered from North Africa to Central Asia, Muslims in South Asia never accounted for more than 25 percent of the population.

iv. The greatest political contribution of the Delhi sultanates was blocking Mongol incursion deeper into South Asia.

> *The Muslim caliphates and sultanates are not "empires" as far as the APWH exam is concerned. The most important Muslim empires were: the Ottoman, based in Turkey but covering much of the Middle East and North Africa (14th–early 20th c); the Safavid, based in Persia (16th–18th c); and the Mughal, based in India (16th–19th c). See Chapter 12.*

C. The Crusades

1. The Crusades were a series of Muslim-Christian clashes over control of Southwest Asia beginning in the late eleventh century and lasting about 200 years.

    i. Religious causes of the Crusades: Christians sought to re-establish their faith in Southwest Asia, which they felt had been pushed aside by Muslims through *jihad*.

    ii. Political and economic causes also contributed to the Crusades. For example, the Byzantine Empire wanted to retake land it had lost to the Seljuk Turks and asked Christians in western Europe for help. Despite a split in Christianity in 1054 that formed the Roman Catholic and Eastern Orthodox churches, the westerners sent both trained forces (knights) and woefully untrained forces (monks and laypeople).

    iii. The greatest economic cause of the Crusades was trade. Europeans were concerned that luxury goods from Asia (spices and silk) would be cut off if the Byzantine capital, Constantinople, came under Muslim control. In addition, some wealthy western Europeans went on crusades to establish trade with Muslim merchants.

2. Results of the Crusades

    i. Militarily, the Europeans gained only small territories along the eastern coast of the Mediterranean. These so-called Crusader states became centers of Christianity and trade with "the East." Jerusalem became a city jointly occupied by Muslims, Jews, and Christians.

c. 600–c. 1450 CE

    ii. Culturally, the Crusades resulted in great advancements for the Europeans, who, for example, rediscovered Roman and Greek literature that Muslim scholars had maintained for centuries.

       ➤ The science, math, and philosophies of those Classical civilizations began an intellectual revival in the fourteenth and fifteenth centuries called the *Renaissance*.

       ➤ This started western Europe on a path toward global hegemony (control) in the nineteenth century.

    iii. Economic results for the Europeans were also good. Spices, foods, silk, cotton, and many other products entered western Europe as never before.

       ➤ The demand for these goods led to an increase in the number of towns along trade routes to the "East" and an increase in wealth in the "West," which led to more trade.

       ➤ Finding alternate and (hopefully) cheaper ways of trading these goods ultimately led to expeditions funded by European monarchs. Christopher Columbus led one of those expeditions.

    iv. Increased contacts between western Europeans and Asians via trade also led to the introduction of unfamiliar diseases into the West. See Chapter 7 for a discussion of the effects of the Black Death.

Test Tip *You've noticed a lot of inclusion of religion with discussions of politics in this chapter. That's how AP World History works—it blends political, social, economic, geographic, and environmental themes throughout the course.*

II. China's Dynasties

A. After the fall of the Han Dynasty (c. 220 CE), regional rulers emerged in China.

1. The next family to reunite much of China was the Sui, followed immediately by the economic golden ages of the Tang and Song dynasties.

2. Throughout history, China's governments combined traditional sources of power (like patriarchy—a male-dominated society) and new methods of rule (like the Tang method of taking a census to establish tax rates).

B. The Sui Dynasty did not last long (581–618 CE), but its emperors' policies did.

1. Public works projects like the Grand Canal and the Great Wall were revived.

2. The Sui reinstituted the Confucian examination system for civil service and Buddhism increased in popularity during this period.

C. The Tang Dynasty (618–907 CE) immediately followed the Sui. Along with the Song Dynasty, it represented the Golden Age of the influence of Chinese culture, economic power, and scientific achievement.

1. The Tang emperors ruled from the world's largest city, Chang'an (modern day Xi'an). More about China's great economic strength will be discussed in the next chapter.

    i. From the Sui to the Tang dynasties, construction on the Great Wall and the Confucian system of civil service exams continued.

    ii. Changes from the Sui to the Tang included the official government rejection of Buddhism and the restoration of Confucianism. In addition, government bureaucracy became more complex.

    iii. The Tang Empire was similar in size and shape to the Han Empire, covering most of modern China and reaching along the Silk Roads into the Tarim basin north of Tibet and India.

        ➤ The Tang leaders expanded the size of their empire in much the same way other societies had: military power, diplomacy, and trade.

➤ The Tang government also raised taxes to pay for its operations. First, they conducted a census to count the people and to find out where people lived, then the government imposed small taxes on cloth and grain.

—In the mid-eighth century CE, the census counted about 50 million people—easily the highest population of any civilization in the world at that time.

—In the early twenty-first century, China still has the most people: over 1.3 billion.

iv. Tang art, especially ceramics, was among the world's most beautiful.

➤ Glazed porcelain horses and other figures were delicate, colorful, and in great demand along the Silk Roads.

➤ Tang technology included printing, gunpowder, medicine, the compass, and ship construction—all of which were far ahead of the rest of the world.

D. The Song Dynasty (960–1279 CE) followed the Tang, which collapsed after floods, famine, pirates, and bandits created great chaos in the empire. Transition from one dynasty to the next was fairly stable because of the people's faith in the mandate of heaven, a belief that heaven would support an emperor as long as he ruled well. If calamity struck and a dynasty fell, the Chinese trusted that a new and better dynasty was on the way.

1. Continuities from the Tang to the Song Dynasty included exports of manufactured goods via the Silk Roads and by sea, continued development of urban centers, and the Confucian examination system.

2. Changes from Tang to Song included the development of Neo-Confucianism and the practice of foot-binding among women.

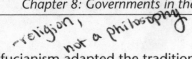

→ religion, not a philosophy

    i.   Neo-Confucianism adapted the traditional, orderly, patriarchal rules of its originator, with influences from Buddhism and Daoism.

    ii.   Confucius had set up a philosophy of societal order, not a religion. His philosophy changed into a popular salvationist faith beginning in the Song Dynasty and was called Neo-Confucianism. It became a religion promising eternal reward. This is another example of cultural blending, which occurs often in major religions.

↳ Syncretism?

  3. One result of the restoration of Confucian morals and its male-first views was the reduction in the status of women during the Song Dynasty.

    i.   The most famous—or infamous—example was the practice of foot-binding. Young girls' feet were folded in half, bones were broken, and wrapped with binding to create a small foot that was thought to be very attractive to men.

    ii.   Foot binding also made it very difficult for women to walk. Women were expected to remain at home and be little more than the property of their fathers or husbands.

III. China's Influence on Korea, Japan, and Vietnam

Sinification is the term used for the spread of Chinese culture. During the Tang and Song Dynasties, China exerted a powerful political and cultural influence over its neighbors, in particular Korea, Japan, and Vietnam.

A. Sinification in Korea affected politics, art, and religion.

  1. The Tang Dynasty conquered Korea—at least, for a while—but found maintaining rule to be difficult, so they removed their military forces from Korea. In return, the Korean Silla dynasty made regular payments of money and goods—tribute—to China.

    2. Impressed by the political and economic success of Tang China, Korean leaders did some cultural borrowing from China.

        i.   Korean scholars traveled to China to consult with Confucian scholars and returned with the latest Chinese books, technology, and ideas.

        ii. Chinese culture in the form of writing, religion (Buddhism), fashion, and architecture made their way into Korea.

        iii. The elite classes of Koreans adopted Confucianism.

B. Sinification in Japan occurred largely voluntarily.

    1. Japan intentionally chose to incorporate important aspects of Chinese civilization. The Chinese never conquered Japan, but the success of China under the Tang Dynasty motivated Japanese emperors to adopt elements of Chinese civilization.

        i.   Chinese writing, bureaucracy, and belief systems were purposely borrowed. In fact, Japan is one of history's greatest cultural borrowers, a practice that continues today.

    2. Buddhism became so popular in Japan that aristocrats feared the power of Buddhists in the government.

    3. Confucianism was another popular belief system borrowed from China.

    4. During the Heian Era in Japan (794–1185 CE), courtly life was an "ultracivilized" aristocracy.

        i.   The details of this life are captured in Lady Murasaki's *The Tale of Genji,* considered to be the world's first novel.

    5. Too much attention on the frivolous life at court led to a loss of power for the emperor and to the establishment of the Shogun, rule by a military strongman.

        i.   The emperor remained, but with a greatly reduced role.

        ii. Japan became a feudal society, similar to western Europe at about the same time, with rich landowners overseeing poor farm workers and obtaining protections from a private army of knights, the *Samurais.*

C. Sinification in Vietnam

1. During the Tang Dynasty, Chinese armies marched into Vietnam but saw only temporary success.

   i. The Vietnamese revolted early and often.

   ii. Women in Vietnam did not accept the Confucian system of male dominance.

2. One benefit the Tang derived from their interaction with Vietnam was a quicker-ripening form of rice. Once they had adopted this from Vietnam, this type of rice became an important part of the Chinese diet, and its population became—and remains—the most numerous in the world.

IV. The Mongols' Large Empires

Some historians have called the Mongols "an unstoppable and bloody tide of horror," while others consider them clever "agents of change." However they have been described over the centuries, it is undeniable that the Mongols had a profound effect on the peoples of Eurasia.

A. From the thirteenth to the fifteenth centuries, Mongol rule stretched from East Asia to eastern Europe.

1. The Mongols were, and remain, pastoralists—nomadic peoples from Mongolia who herd sheep; yaks; goats; cattle; and, more importantly, horses.

   i. In the early thirteenth century, led by Chinggis (Genghis) Khan, the Mongols swept south into China, eventually reaching—and ending—the Song Dynasty.

   ii. After merciless military campaigns that brought them to power, the Mongols made Beijing their capital and ended the Confucian examination system.

   iii. The Mongols allowed foreigners, especially Arab Muslims, to administer the government.

   iv. Chinggis Khan also marched west toward Persia, setting the stage for future assaults by his descendants.

C. 600–C. 1450 CE

v. Chinggis's grandson, Kublai Khan, established the Yuan Dynasty in China, which lasted until 1368, when rebellions drove the Mongols to their homeland on the steppes of Mongolia.

B. The Pax Mongolica

1. The Mongols favored trade, and when they took over the regions along the Silk Roads, the routes were so free of bandits that historians still speak of a Pax Mongolica ("Mongol peace").

   i. The Pax Mongolica came at a high price.

   ➤ Cities that opposed the Mongols disappeared from the map.

   ➤ Baghdad's leaders resisted Mongol attacks in 1258 and 200,000 people died. The Abbasid Empire died with them.

   ➤ Central Asia lost as many as three-quarters of its population to Mongol destruction.

   ➤ It is estimated that China's population declined by half during the Yuan Dynasty.

   ii. Historians debate how much responsibility the Mongols had for all these deaths, arguing that epidemic diseases and famines could have contributed to the totals.

C. Expansion

1. Through these conquests, the Mongol Empire expanded quickly—so quickly that one man could not oversee it all.

   i. The Mongol Empire divided into regional khanates after Chinggis died, and these khanates reached to eastern Europe, Central Asia, and Southwest Asia.

   ii. The Mongols' further advance was stopped in modern-day Israel by Mamluk warriors from Egypt.

2. The Russians called the Mongols *The Golden Horde*.

    i.   After their destructive invasion, the Mongols reached an agreement with local Russian leaders who collected tribute to send to their Mongol masters.

    ii. This tribute arrangement lasted 200 years until Ivan the Great, prince of Moscow, led a successful and lasting revolt against the Mongols in 1480.

3. Over time, the people in all Mongol khanates rebelled and Mongol rule came to an end. But the legacy of the Mongols remained.

    i.   They controlled the largest empire the world has ever seen.

    ii. They allowed freedom of religion in the areas they conquered.

    iii. The Mughal Empire of South Asia took its name from the Mongols.

    iv. Increased trade because of the Pax Mongolica resulted in the rapid spread of the Black Death all across the khanates and into western Europe.

V. Muslim and Christian Kingdoms Thrive in Africa

A. Sudanic States

1. Southwest of the Sahara in the African grasslands called the Sahel, the Muslim kingdoms of Ghana, Songhay, and Mali exported salt, gold, and animal skins across the desert via camel caravans and connected into the Afro-Eurasia network of exchange.

2. These Sudanic states developed major trade and education centers like Timbuktu, D'jenne (Jenne), and Gao.

3. The borders of these civilizations were often difficult to define and sometimes overlapped.

c. 600–c. 1450 CE

B. Ethiopia

1. Before the arrival of Islam into Africa, Christianity was the major religion of Egypt, Nubia, and Ethiopia.

2. Over time, Christians became a minority compared to Muslims in Egypt and Nubia, but Ethiopia remains largely Christian in the twenty-first century.

3. In the thirteenth century, King Lalibela of Ethiopia had a series of Christian churches carved out of rock to symbolize his kingdom's unshakable faith in that religion.

4. One of Ethiopia's major exports was coffee, which was especially valued in the Muslim world during this era.

Economic Activity and Its Effects
c. 600–c. 1450 CE

As you've learned by now, economic activity, such as the sale of agricultural products and the exchange of goods through trade, is a very important topic in AP World History, and their effects can last for centuries. In this chapter, you will study changes in agriculture and manufacturing and their effects on trade, cities, and labor in the era c. 600–c. 1450 CE.

I. New Developments in Agriculture and Manufacturing

A. The introduction of new crops and planting methods led to increases in farm production.

1. In the last chapter, you learned that China imported a type of rice from Vietnam that greatly increased China's food supply. They weren't alone in developing new methods of growing food.

   i. In the Americas, the Aztecs developed a unique system of agriculture—the *chinampas* field system to feed the large population of the Aztec capital Tenochtitlán, which was situated in the middle of Lake Texcoco in central Mexico.

   ii. The *chinampas* system called for large human-made, floating "islands" of crops to be constructed in the lake and the canals. Workers wove huge flat baskets and piled mud on top of them. They then planted crops, such as maize (American corn), in the soil. The plants were watered by their roots, which grew through the baskets into the water.

2. In western Europe, several developments from exchanges with Muslims in North Africa and Southwest Asia increased crop production.

   i. These developments included the horse collar, the three-field system of crop rotation, and horseshoes.

      ➤ The horse collar made it possible for a horse to pull a plow.

      ➤ Rotating varieties of crops in a field increased crop yield because the soil's nutrients were less depleted.

      ➤ The horseshoe protected the horses' hooves, so horses did not need to be replaced so often.

   ii. With these developments in place, farming expenses decreased and farmers had more money to invest in additional land and crops.

3. All of these developments, which the Chinese and Muslim Arabs had learned centuries before the Europeans, resulted in increased amounts of food for Europeans, so populations increased and cities grew.

B. The manufacture and export of products from China, Persia, and India increased.

   1. As you read in Chapter 8, China produced some of the world's most beautiful ceramic works for export, such as small porcelain statues of people and animals; porcelain tableware; and, of course, silk.

   2. Persia manufactured ceramic goods for export as well, but also exported hand-made Persian rugs; items made of copper, glass, and brass; Islamic-themed art; and silk. They learned how to process silk from the Chinese.

   3. India also produced brass items, such as Buddhist religious art. They also grew cotton and wove cotton cloth.

   4. All these products were exchanged throughout Afro-Eurasia along the Silk Roads and Indian Ocean trading networks.

See previous chapters for lists of agricultural products that were exchanged along regional trade routes in this and earlier periods. Combine those lists with the manufactured items named above and you'll have plenty of essay material for questions about the Afro-Eurasian trading network by sea and on land.

II. **Cities Decline and Then Revive**

A. When the classical empires fell, cities declined.

  1. Political order and economic vitality in cities were adversely affected by the fall of the classical empires by 600 CE.

   i. When invaders swept through declining empires, they often targeted the riches of the cities and killed much of the population. Many citizens fled to the countryside, which was often overlooked by the invaders.

   ii. Unfortunately for merchants and consumers, cities were linked by trade routes. When bandits made trade routes more dangerous, trade declined and hurt the cities' economies.

   iii. Finally, diseases that devastated the falling empires were particularly destructive in cities because higher population densities meant a quicker transfer of disease. For example, of the 80,000 or so people living in Florence, Italy, when the Black Death hit in the mid-fourteenth century, approximately 50,000 died.

B. Cities revived over time in the Post-Classical Era.

  1. As new governments gradually replaced those that collapsed in the Classical period, stability and safety slowly returned and cities rebounded.

  2. Several factors contributed to urban revival:

   i. Because of the return of military forces from the new governments, trade routes became safer, and invasions from nomads like the Mongols ended.

C. 600–C. 1450 CE

    ii.   Safer trade routes led to more jobs in the cities, attracting still more people.

    iii. New food-growing methods, such as crop rotation (discussed above) meant more food was available to feed people in the cities.

    iv. The climate changed. There was a mini-Ice Age in the Post-Classical Era, but global temperatures began to rise in the latter half of the era. This resulted in increased food production—good for trade and commerce.

    v.   In western Europe, agricultural serfs started to gain their freedom after the catastrophe of the Black Death. Many of them left the feudal life and moved into the cities.

C. The Post-Classical Era saw the rise of many significant cities that made significant contributions to societies.

  1. In the Tang and Song Dynasties, China had the world's largest, richest, most technologically advanced, and beautiful cities. Examples include the following:

    i.   The Tang capital, Chang'an, with 2 million people, had a sectioned-off government zone, elaborate gardens, suburbs where city workers lived, and a busy commercial area.

    ii. Hangzhou, with more than 1.5 million people, was crossed by canals and bridges, had ten market centers that sold goods throughout Afro-Eurasia, in theaters, parks, restaurants, and museums. The Italian merchant/explorer Marco Polo called Hangzhou the "best city in the world."

  2. In Mesoamerica, the Aztecs called their capital of Tenochtitlán the "foundation of heaven."

    i.   This title marks a big contrast to the cities in China, where there was no religious significance tied to cities, but it is similar to the veneration given Christian cities like Rome, and Muslim cities like Mecca.

    ii. The central area of the city of Tenochtitlán housed government buildings and religious structures. The great pyramid and two temples stood above all other buildings in Tenochtitlán. In addition, there were markets, gardens, and a zoo. As noted above, the most unusual thing about the Aztec capital was its position in the middle of a huge lake; still, it was able to maintain a population of about 150,000, larger than most European cities at the time.

3. In Europe, one of the great cities was Venice, uniquely positioned on 117 islands in the northeast Italian peninsula.

   i. Venice was a major trade hub linking Europe to Africa, Asia, and especially the Byzantine Empire.

   ii. Because of its strong economy, Venice became a powerful city-state in this era, with its own formidable military forces. City-states were still around by the mid-sixteenth century, even though their heyday was way back in the Classical Era.

   iii. Venice exported Christian-themed paintings and statuary.

   iv. Venice had close political and economic ties to Constantinople, another formidable European city of the age. Marco Polo (see Chapter 7) was from Venice, so when he complimented the cities he visited in China, it was high praise indeed.

Test Tip

The AP World History curriculum expects you to be able to explain the political, economic, social, and cultural contributions of important cities in every era. See Chapters 7, 8, and 9 for examples in the era c. 600–c. 1450.

III. Old and New Types of Labor

A. Agricultural labor, including work by serfs, free peasants, nomadic pastoralists (see Chapter 3), and slaves remained the main forms of labor.

c. 600–c. 1450 CE

1. Governments continued to force workers to complete public works projects, such as building the Great Wall in China or road building in Europe.

2. Manufacturing had a growing need for laborers.

B. New types of agricultural labor arose in this era.

1. Coerced labor—a world history term for "forced labor"— now included serfdom in western and eastern Europe and Japan.

   i. Serfs differed from slaves in that they were not sold by individuals. They were "tied to the land," meaning that they generally stayed on the same land regardless of who the landowner was.

   ii. Like slaves, serfs received no pay, but they also did not pay taxes.

   iii. In the feudal system in western Europe and Japan, most farm laborers were serfs, but by the end of this era, serfdom was in decline in western Europe.

   iv. In Russia in eastern Europe, many free peasants actually volunteered to become serfs to avoid paying taxes like the free peasants.

2. In the Inca Empire in Andean South America, the *mita* system was similar to the kinds of coerced labor the Chinese and European landlords employed to build public works projects. In the next era, Europeans who conquered the Inca adapted the *mita* system to their own benefit.

3. Peasants in the Americas and throughout Afro-Eurasia revolted against forced labor from time to time. Landowners and the government suppressed these revolts, which resulted in lower agricultural output.

4. In China, peasant revolts were seen as a sign the emperor might be losing his mandate of heaven.

5. The revival of empires meant an increased demand for slaves to work in agriculture because stable governments led to safer trade routes that, in turn, increased trade, including trade of agricultural products.

    i.   The new empires expanded their militaries that demanded slaves to work in transportation and other services.

    ii.   Africa and eastern Europe were the chief sources for slaves. In fact, the word *slave* comes from the Slavic peoples of eastern Europe.

> The AP World History exam frequently includes questions about forms of agricultural labor such as slavery, serfdom, and indentured servants throughout history. See Chapter 11 for a discussion of indentured servitude.

IV. Changes in Gender Relations and Family Life

A. Status

1. Through most of history, one's status in society was usually determined at birth. In South Asia, the caste system determined your place in society. The social class you were born into was almost always the social class you died in.

2. In the Byzantine and Ottoman empires, one could climb the social ladder through military service or increase one's chances of economic status by becoming a successful merchant.

B. Patriarchy

1. Patriarchy—or male-dominated society—continued as an historical theme in the era c. 600–c. 1450.

2. In Tang and Song China, women's status deteriorated, and across Dar al-Islam, traditional Muslim views of women generally continued.

3. There were exceptions. Mongol and Vietnamese women refused to accept the Chinese cultural expectation of foot-binding. Some Vietnamese women led revolts against Chinese occupation of their lands.

4. Another exception to patriarchy in China was Empress Wu Zetian. *She* was an emperor of China early in the Post-Classical Era.

PERIOD 4

GLOBAL INTERACTIONS

c. 1450–c. 1750 CE

The Development of Global Networks
c. 1450–c. 1750 CE

We have at last arrived at the time when we can talk about truly global history! In the era c.1450–c.1750, the Americas and Oceania (Australia, New Zealand, and the Pacific islands) joined Afro-Eurasia in networks of exchange. The encounters between the people from Europe and the Americas had profound social, political, economic, demographic, and environmental effects on both sides of the Atlantic, and quickly, the world.

I. European Exploration Expands

A. Factors That Led the Europeans to Cross the Atlantic to the Americas

1. Advances in European ship design and navigation

   i. Benefits to Europe from trade with Asia by the end of the previous era included not only spices, but also technology. Some European kings were quick to use the newly acquired methods in shipbuilding and navigation to expand their new kingdoms.

   ii. The compass, more accurate maps, the astrolabe (used to determine latitude), improved ship design including better rudders and sails on ships called caravels—all technology transferred from Asia—contributed to western Europe's ability to make long-distance sailing expeditions.

2. Europeans desired to spread the Christian faith.

   i. Motivated by competition from the Muslim faith, western European Christians—especially those of

Portugal and Spain, who had recently completed a *reconquista* ("reconquering") of the Iberian peninsula from Muslim control—sought to spread their gospel to new areas. They targeted South and East Asia, where conversion had thus far been limited. Expeditions always carried missionaries along.

ii. Changes in Christianity sparked additional motivation to carry the Gospel.

➤ Incentive to expand the Roman Catholic faith came from Catholic nations such as Spain, Portugal, and France.

➤ The Protestant Reformation of the early 1500s split the Western Christian church, but it also caused a renewed missionary vigor among the Catholic monarchs in western Europe who now saw not only Muslims as competitors for the world's souls, but also Protestants.

➤ It became a matter of great importance for Catholic monarchs to evangelize the world before Protestants could.

3. Trade was also a major motivator. The Europeans saw how the flow of silk, technology, and spices westward from Asia increased wealth in Europe tremendously, triggered the Renaissance, and sparked a revival of cities. They hoped to increase their wealth with trade goods from the Americas.

4. Why Western Europe and Not Eastern Europe?

i. Like the nations in western Europe, Russia also had access to the new shipping technology and sent ships north into the Arctic Ocean seeking a route to East Asia. Icy conditions, however, made that passage impossible.

ii. At the same time, Russia was expanding its *land* empire across Siberia and did not enter the Pacific until the seventeenth century.

iii. European rivals closer to the Atlantic had geographic advantages when it came to exploring the Americas.

iv. Other nations in central and eastern Europe had limited access to the sea and/or were not yet organized well enough to send expensive expeditions around the world.

5. Why Not China?

    i. In the early fifteenth century, China sent fleets of ships to the Indian Ocean region as a show of might and because of sheer curiosity about the world beyond its borders. They sent enormous "treasure ships" that were 400 feet long and carried thousands of sailors commanded by the Chinese Muslim Admiral Zheng He. (Columbus's biggest ship, the *Santa Maria*, was about 70 feet long.)

    ii. Zheng He brought back to the Ming court all kinds of animals, plants, goods, and people from Africa and India, but after 28 years and three explorations, the Ming emperor's advisers convinced him that the expeditions were too expensive and that China had little to gain from them. After all, they reasoned, the Middle Kingdom was the greatest in the world. Thus, as the Portuguese began a series of explorations along Africa's west coast, China chose to withdraw its fleet from the Indian Ocean. China had the capacity to sail in force anywhere it wanted to, and refused.

II. Portugal Leads the Way to New Lands; Spain Follows

A. Geography and European Exploration

1. Why were Portugal and Spain the first European nations to venture south (Portugal) and west (Spain) into the Atlantic?

    i. First, geography. Both Portugal and Spain have coasts that jutted farther into the Atlantic than other European nations. Portugal's proximity to Africa made southern exploration a logical target.

    ii. Second, the newly united nation-state of Spain had just completed a centuries-long campaign to restore the Iberian Peninsula to Christian control. Thus, Spain's leaders experienced a great deal of patriotic energy and

C. 1450–C. 1750 CE

were willing to spend money to expand their economic, religious, and political influence beyond their borders.

   iii. Third, geography played another important part because Italy's position in the middle of the Mediterranean meant it was ideally situated to be at the center of exchanges between western Europe and the "East"—the ports of the eastern Mediterranean and their sought-after goods. Portugal and Spain wanted to bypass the Italian control of trade between East and West, so they searched for alternate routes to Asia, for instance, around Africa (Portugal) and west across the Atlantic (Spain).

B. Portugal Charts the Western Coast of Africa.

  1. Portugal's Prince Henry the Navigator sent ship after ship down the western coast of Africa looking for a route to the Indies so that his nation could benefit from direct trade with South Asia.

    i. Along the way, the Portuguese charted the Madeira Islands and the Azores Islands.

    ii. In 1488, Portuguese ships reached and rounded the Cape of Good Hope in South Africa and for the next ten years, Portuguese and Arab merchants interacted in the Indian Ocean area.

    iii. In 1498, Vasco da Gama succeeded in making it to India and returned to Portugal with spices and other goods. The Portuguese finally established their link to the East. But, had the Spanish beaten them?

C. The Spanish Sought a Different Route to the East.

  1. The Spanish didn't have much choice because the Portuguese and Italians had already claimed their own routes.

    i. Since the only known landmass on Earth was Afro-Eurasia, sailing west across the Atlantic seemed logical in that it would bring a ship straight to the islands near India, the Indies, and maybe even China ("Cathay").

    ii.   Columbus convinced the Spanish royals to fund an expedition for God and for gold—in this case, "gold" meant anything of great value, like spices, silk, or even gold. For himself, Columbus sought glory. (Thus we get the famous "Three G's of Exploration"—God, glory, and gold.)

    iii. If Columbus made it to the East and back, he would put Spain ahead of Portugal, who in 1492, was still trying to find India.

2. The Spanish thought Columbus had made it—but, of course, he was in the Americas. Eventually the place where he did land—Cuba and the surrounding islands—were labeled the "West Indies" and its people were called "Indians". That shows you how much Spain was aiming for the prize of South Asia's Spice Islands, the *real* Indies.

    i.   After Spain began to accumulate great agricultural and mining wealth from the Americas, it seemed Columbus's voyages were not the "mistake" everyone initially thought they had been.

III. The Columbian Exchange's Effect on the World

Historians refer to the transfer of animals, plants, diseases, and people that resulted from contacts between Europeans and Amerindians (Native Americans in both North and South America) as the *Columbian Exchange* after the explorer Columbus, who started the process in 1492. Note that this was a two-way exchange to and from the Americas.

A. Animals and Plants of the Columbian Exchange

1. From Afro-Eurasia to the Americas: Europeans brought horses, pigs, chickens, cows, sugarcane, bananas, wheat, and rice, to name just a few. Effects on the environment were enormous.

    i.   The introduction of horses to the Americas changed the cultures of almost every Native American group.

          ii.   Sugarcane plantations throughout the Caribbean helped create rich European kingdoms, and resulted in the importation of slaves from Africa.

    2. From the Americas to Afro-Eurasia: Europeans returned with few animals that had a global impact, but among plants, they brought back potatoes, tomatoes, tobacco, American corn (maize), cocoa, and chili peppers as well as other peppers.

          i.   The potato became popular in Europe—it stored well on ships and grew in a wide variety of soils and climates.

          ii.   Maize became a staple in both Africa and China.

          iii. These American foods created unprecedented population growth wherever they were planted.

B. Diseases Resulting from the Columbian Exchange

    1. The greatest effect on the people of the Americas was the introduction of diseases that had not existed before the arrival of the Europeans.

          i.   Smallpox, in particular, eradicated whole villages of native people, creating a demographic catastrophe that has not been equaled in all of history. It is estimated that approximately 90 percent of the population of the Americas died from these newly introduced diseases.

          ii.   This depopulation created huge open spaces for Europeans to conquer and settle with little resistance.

C. People Migrated to the Americas During the Columbian Exchange.

    1. Most people migrated voluntarily, but many Africans were forcibly taken to the Americas to serve as slaves. Some Europeans (from the Spanish-held Canary Islands) were also resettled to the Americas against their will as colonists and/ or indentured servants.

    2. Spanish explorers were not settlers and few women made the early voyages. Mixed-race children were born out of relationships between Spaniards and native women. Slowly,

European women made the dangerous trip to the Americas, and European-only families began to form. Thus, a new social hierarchy was created, with skin color being the determining factor in status. (See Chapter 11.)

3. Europeans created large, highly profitable sugarcane plantations in the Caribbean but, because of the virtual elimination of natives, a great shortage of labor resulted.

    i. Portugal was first among European nations to enslave Africans along Africa's Atlantic coast, and haul them to their sugarcane plantations in Brazil.

    ii. Spain followed, buying Africans from merchants along the "Slave Coast" and transporting them in packed ships across the Atlantic (the Middle Passage) to the Caribbean to work producing sugar.

D. Religions of the Columbian Exchange

1. Christian missionaries accompanied explorers and settlers to the Americas.

    i. In their zeal to spread the holy word, Catholic clergy in both the Portuguese and Spanish territories held mass baptisms with little religious instruction.

    ii. This meant the traditions of the original faiths of the natives continued with Christian beliefs woven in.

E. Precious Metals of the Columbian Exchange

1. Gold from central Mexico went straight into the Spanish monarch's treasury, but it was silver from Peru that became the global metal of exchange.

    i. Silver from the Americas was traded for Asian spices, silk, and all the other commodities Europeans had come to desire.

    ii. Japan was brought into this network because it, too, had silver mines. China and India were, of course, on the receiving end of most of the silver.

    iii. For the first time, a global network of exchange was established.

c. 1450–c. 1750 CE

IV. Latin America and the Atlantic World

A. Social Shifts in Latin America

1. Latin American society was the result of the blending of European, African, and Native American cultures. Food, faith, family structure, and racial identities were affected by the contacts among these people over many centuries.

B. Economics and the Atlantic World

1. The Atlantic World is described by the interaction among the four continents on both sides of the Atlantic: North America, South America, Europe, and Africa.

   i. Latin America is, of course, also part of the Atlantic World.

   ii. England, France, and, to a lesser extent, the Netherlands (Holland/the Dutch) followed Spain and Portugal in establishing colonies in the Americas. All held islands in the Caribbean with sugar plantations and competed with each other in that global market.

2. The thirteen English colonies

   i. For most of this era, the English, French, and Dutch colonies along the North Atlantic coast of North America were an afterthought. One historian called them a "colonial backwater." That's because they were not a big deal compared to the wealth of metals and sugar coming out of Latin America.

   ii. The biggest economic contribution from the colonies of *upper* North America—remember, the Caribbean and Mexico are considered part of North America, too— was fish. Cod was enormously popular among people on both sides of the Atlantic. Its presence off the coast of Massachusetts, near Cape Cod, made European monarchs give colonization there a try.

3. *Triangle Trade* is a term familiar to most AP World History students. Sugar, rum (which comes from fermented sugarcane), and cod were shipped to Europe and exchanged for silver, which was shipped to Africa and exchanged for slaves. Slaves were then sent to the Americas. (The reality was much more complicated than this simple description, but the term *Triangle Trade* remains in the AP World History lexicon.)

4. *Mercantilism* is another very important term to know for the AP World History exam.

   i.   European monarchs used raw materials from the colonies to manufacture products from those materials to sell globally. The idea was to have a positive balance of trade.

   ii. Governments put taxes—tariffs—on imported products from rival nations. They also went into business with private companies who traded globally. The British East India Company (EIC) is an important example.

   iii. With the cooperation of the government, the British EIC made and enforced its own laws, approved ship schedules and cargoes, and negotiated commerce agreements with rulers all over the world.

V. **Continuities in the Global Networks of Exchange**

The era c. 1450–c. 1750 isn't "all Atlantic, all the time." And it isn't only about change, either, although the changes you've learned about were vast.

A. Continuities in Religion

   1. Islam continued to spread as it had in the earlier era into sub-Saharan regions and into East and Southeast Asia, including parts of the Philippines.

c. 1450–c. 1750 CE

2. Buddhism continued to move across Southeast Asia and into parts of Central Asia.

3. Hinduism continued to be the core religion of India.

4. People yet to be contacted by Buddhists, Christians, or Muslims continued to practice their indigenous faiths.

B. Continuities in Trade and Agriculture

1. In the Indian Ocean region, trade among the traditional participants from East Africa, South Asia, Southeast Asia, and East Asia continued.

2. European merchants learned they could only join in when they cooperated with local rulers of port cities in this region because they were unable to dominate this long-lasting trade culture.

3. The volume of Atlantic World trade eventually surpassed that of the Indian Ocean network by the middle of this era.

4. Most people around the world remained farmers in this era. Many were subsistence farmers—that is, they grew enough for their family with a little left over to sell.

5. Other farmers grew a single crop for a landowner who exported the food—the beginnings of commercial farming.

6. Changes in crops that were grown occurred because of the influx of new foods from the Americas—corn in China, for example.

C. Continuities in Migrations

1. On the eve of European contacts, migration by indigenous peoples had largely ended, reaching the islands of Hawaii by c. 900, with a possible second wave of Tahitian settlers in c. 1300.

2. In Southeast Africa, Bantu-speaking peoples built the city complex of Great Zimbabwe.

Changes to Societies and Methods of Production
c. 1450–c. 1750 CE

As you might expect, contacts among the Americas, Oceania, and Afro-Eurasia had profound effects that still resonate today. In the era c. 1450–c. 1750, societies changed and so did the means of producing goods. Not everything changed, of course. Continuities remained in social structures; for example, elites still ran the show everywhere. In China, one continuity was that patriarchy remained strong.

I. **New Political and Economic Elite Groups**

A. Political Elites

   1. China

      i.   The Manchus defeated the Ming leadership and established themselves as the new elite ruling class.

      ii. The Manchus were from the northeast corner of East Asia, namely, Manchuria.

      iii. Although they established a new dynasty—the Qing (1644–1912)—they remained a minority ethnic group in the land they ruled.

      iv. The Qing adopted the Chinese language, Confucian philosophy, and the Chinese bureaucracy, and continued the mandate of heaven.

   2. Latin America

      i.   The new ruling class in Latin America was the *Creole elites*.

    ii. Settlers in the Americas who were born in Spain or Portugal were called the *Peninsulares* because they came from the Iberian Peninsula. They were at the top of Latin American society and government.

    iii. Next on the societal pyramid were the *Creoles*—those Europeans born in the Americas.

    iv. Over time, as the number of Peninsulares faded and the number of Creoles increased, the distinction between the two faded as well.

    v. Below the elites in Latin America were a wide variety of mixed-race peoples, called *mestizos*. Essentially, the more European "blood" a person had (or, conveniently, the whiter the skin), the higher they were on the Latin American social ladder. People with strong Amerindian or African features tended to be lower on the social ladder.

3. North American British and French colonies

    i. In the thirteen English colonies or New France—from northeast Canada into the Ohio River valley—there was much less mixing of races.

    ii. European elites, such as large landowners or wealthy merchants, established themselves at the top of colonial society, and other "whites" such as small farmers, craftspeople, and indentured servants were lower on the socioeconomic pyramid.

    iii. No matter how poor, a white person was always above Indians and African slaves.

B. Economic Elites

1. In Europe, new economic elites rose out of the merchant class. Entrepreneurs who did well in the global trade game were rewarded with financial success and social status.

2. In China, merchants were considered to be of low social status, but they enjoyed the benefits of wealth.

3. Outside China, wealthy merchants were often members of the social elite in every major port city in the world.

II. **Developments in Christianity and European Science**

A. Latin Americans Synthesized Catholicism and Local Traditional Faiths.

    1. One of the requirements of a global religion is that it adapt to local customs. Christianity, in its Catholic form, did so in Latin America.

    2. With official sponsorship from both the church and European rulers, missionaries in Latin America had great success, but the religion that emerged after encounters with traditional beliefs was not the same as when it arrived from Europe.

        i. In Mexico, for example, many Christian saints took on the same responsibilities as the precolonial gods they replaced. As had been done before Christianity arrived, offerings were made and votive candles lit in prayer asking for divine intercession.

        ii. In the Caribbean, a mix of African religions and Christianity merged to produce *Vodun*, or voodoo.

B. Reformations Divided the Christian Church and Revived its Missionary Activity.

    1. At the same time that western Europe was settling the Americas and establishing trade in the Indian Ocean, the Christian church in western Europe was becoming unsettled.

    2. A Roman Catholic priest and scholar named Martin Luther began the Protestant Reformation in the sixteenth century, challenging the authority and lifestyle of some Catholic leaders, including the pope. He rejected many teachings of the Catholic tradition.

        i. "Protestant" because he and his followers protested what they saw as abuses of power and privilege practiced by some in Catholic leadership.

        ii. "Reformation" because Luther believed his ideas would reform Christianity. For example, he rejected the Catholic teachings of the day such as the spiritual

C. 1450–C. 1750 CE

superiority of the clergy and the sale of "indulgences" to the faithful. *Indulgences* were documents proclaiming that sins were forgiven.

iii. Luther's concept of the equality of all believers before God struck a chord with many in Europe, and his ideas became popular among political leaders. Henry VIII of England broke with the church in Rome and established the Anglican (English) Church because of Luther's ideas.

iv. What Protestantism did *not* offer was an official role in the church for women, as Catholicism did. Women held leadership positions within the Catholic Church serving as nuns in convents and schools.

3. The Catholic Church responded to the Protestant Reformation with a reformation of its own. Some of Luther's objections, such as the buying of indulgences, were addressed.

i. The greatest global effect of the Catholic Reformation was the formation of the Jesuits.

➤ The Jesuits were a group of priests with a strong missionary zeal.

➤ They called themselves the "Army of the Pope."

➤ They were particularly effective in winning conversions in Latin America and in reversing gains made by Protestants in Poland.

4. Jesuit missionaries in China had a different kind of success— not so much spiritual because relatively few Chinese accepted Christianity, but rather academic and scientific.

i. The Ming and Qing emperors appointed Jesuit diplomats from Europe to head the Bureau of Astronomy.

ii. Jesuits brought mathematical and scientific information from Europe that impressed the Chinese—not an easy thing to do.

iii. This marked a turning point in global leadership in technology from East to West in this era.

> *Questions about the globalization of religions and their effects are common on the AP World History exam.*

C. Europe's Scientific Revolution

1. Since the Renaissance, European scientists had been accumulating and refining scientific and mathematical data garnered along trade routes through interaction with Muslim and Chinese scholars.

   i. The monarchs of European nations in the fifteenth through seventeenth centuries (such as Spain, Portugal, England, and France) sponsored men and women who conducted scientific research with the hope that new technology might give their country a competitive edge in world markets.

      ➤ For example, after Columbus returned from the Americas, monarchs started funding experiments designed to determine longitude at sea. Determining which longitude a ship was on wasn't figured out until the mid-eighteenth century when British clock maker John Harrison claimed his government's prize for inventing an accurate sea chronometer that quickly determined longitude.

2. The Scientific Revolution's long-term effects on Western society was to reduce people's faith in divine explanations of life's mysteries. The Christian church still had millions of followers, but Westerners began to look to and depend more on science for answers to society's challenges. That tendency led to the Industrial Revolution.

III. **Developments in Labor Systems**

The inclusion of the Americas and Oceania into the global systems of exchange expanded the world economy. This change had a major effect on labor systems around the world.

A. Peasant Labor Increased in Russia, India, and China.

1. As a result of increased requirements for goods to trade on the new global market, Russia expanded into Siberia and began to export valuable furs, especially to the newly rich European market.

   i. Peasants in Siberia were involved in the trapping and processing of the furs and were also involved with farming large tracts of land owned by Russia's elite class.

   ii. The potato, imported from Peru, became a staple of the Russian diet.

2. In India, hand-woven cotton products like muslin—a delicate cotton fabric—were produced by peasant men and women for export throughout Asia and Europe.

3. In China, large numbers of peasants produced silk, which involved cultivating silk worms, extracting the silk, and weaving it. As in the Classical Era, these products were popular throughout Eurasia.

B. Slavery Intensified in Africa and Greatly Affected Its Population.

1. In Africa, the practice of slavery continued, and the exportation of slaves to the Americas by Europeans and north into the Mediterranean and Indian Ocean area by Muslim Arabs intensified because of the need for labor in the new global economy.

   i. Slaves sent to the Americas worked under harsh conditions on sugar plantations in the Caribbean region and in Brazil.

   ii. One indication of the harsh conditions on sugar plantations was that life expectancy was brief—three years on average, according to studies.

2. The massive loss of people out of Africa to slavery—mostly men—had a significant impact on African demography. Population declined and the once-patriarchal social structure was severely disrupted.

C. The *Encomienda* and *Mita* Systems Supplemented Slavery in Latin America.

   1. Spanish colonists used Amerindians who survived the disease pandemics for their labor needs.

      i. Under the *encomienda* system, the crown granted conquistadors and settlers large numbers of native laborers to work the land or, in the case of Peru, the world's largest silver mine at Potosi.

   2. The Incan *mita* system required its population to do public works service. It was adapted by the Spanish to become a system of forced labor.

      i. Complaints of abuse by church and some government officials in Latin America led the crown in Spain to end these systems by the early eighteenth century.

      ii. One well-known advocate for the welfare of the Incan people was the monk Bartolomé de las Casas.

D. Indentured Servitude

   1. In the Americas, Europeans hired indentured servants when slaves were not readily available.

      i. In the English colonies of North America, an indentured servant from England was "hired" by a sponsor in the colonies to work with no pay for about seven years.

      ii. An indentured servant might learn a trade as a craftsperson or as a domestic servant, but the most common duty was working as an agricultural laborer.

      iii. Slavery existed in these colonies, but the vast majority of African slaves were sent to the Caribbean or Brazil.

      iv. At the end of servitude, an indentured servant (assuming he or she had survived) was free of obligations to his or her master.

      v. Thousands of people migrated from England to its colonies in North America as indentured servants.

Test Tip

Changes in labor systems during this era is a frequently tested theme on the AP World History exam.

c. 1450–c. 1750 CE

Developments
in Governments
c. 1450–c. 1750 CE

As in every era, emperors and kings sought to strengthen their power through religion, laws, military force, and economic policies. Some were more successful than others. Meanwhile, in the era c. 1450–c. 1750, some new states arose and others collapsed.

I. Existing Governments Maintain or Increase Their Power

A. China

1. The Qing government was concerned with Russia's rising power to the west and a revival of the Mongols to the north.

   i. In the late seventeenth and early eighteenth centuries, the Qing military went on campaigns to add land in Central Asia to separate China from Russia.

   ii. The Qing military also conducted campaigns in Mongolia to end the threat of any future invasions from the Mongols.

   iii. China was now one of the great land empires. It added the island of Taiwan in the East China Sea to its empire in the late seventeenth century.

2. In general, the Qing did not force the peoples they conquered to adopt Chinese practices. Instead they allowed local rulers to keep ruling, as long as they obeyed Qing policies.

3. The Qing were also tolerant of local faiths and customs.

      i.   They did limit the movements of pastoral herders, significantly reducing the number of people who continued that way of life.

      ii. The Qing also allowed the trade routes along the Silk Roads to wither away, preferring ocean trade to camel caravans over land.

B. Russia

  1. Russia was the other great land empire of Asia. The Ottoman Empire and the Mughal Empire were significant in their respective regions, but neither could match the size and strength of the huge land empires of Russia and China in this era.

  2. Russia's entry into world affairs began with Ivan the Great, who ran off the last of the Mongol rulers in the late fifteenth century.

      i.   From that point on, Russian leaders expanded their territory through conquest, first to the east and then to the south and west. The largest area was to the east across Siberia.

         ➤ In the sixteenth century, Ivan the Terrible began a conquest of Siberia that continued for one hundred years.

         ➤ From the late seventeenth century through the late eighteenth century, Peter the Great and Catherine the Great added territories north of the Black and Caspian seas. Russian migrants flooded into these areas, greatly changing the cultural makeup of each of these regions.

      ii. Like China, the Russian Empire ended the era of the nomadic people—it insisted on farming instead of pastoralism.

      iii. Like the Chinese in Mongolia and Central Asia, and the Spanish and Portuguese in Latin America, Russia imposed requirements for local peasants to build roads and perform other public works projects.

iv. Like China—but unlike Latin America—Russia generally maintained a policy of religious toleration in the regions they conquered.

3. Czars Peter the Great and Catherine the Great not only expanded the Russian Empire's landholdings, they also actively sought to make Russia a "modern" nation along the lines of those in western Europe at the time. They were moderately successful on some fronts.

   i. Peter built a new capital city, St. Petersburg (so humble of him to give it that name), which was modeled after the capitals of western Europe.

   ii. Peter and Catherine modernized the military and—like the Qing and other Chinese dynasties—invited foreign experts to advise the royal court.

   iii. Catherine famously proclaimed Russia to be a European nation. This settled (at least for Russian foreign policy) the question of which direction the government would make a priority, Asia or Europe. Russia's empire occupied both, and in fact, was mostly in Asia.

   iv. Catherine also invited foreigners to settle in Russia and offered incentives for them to do so. Thousands of immigrants, especially from central Europe, took advantage of her offer. This policy was similar to the United States' granting tracts of free land in the Midwest in the nineteenth century.

4. Even after decades of "westernization" by Peter and Catherine, two major institutions carried over unchanged into the nineteenth century in Russia: serfdom and absolute monarchy.

   i. Neither leader ended serfdom (although western Europe had done so in the fifteenth century) nor did they take steps to limit the czar's authority by allowing a constitution or by granting power to their parliament, as England had done.

c. 1450–c. 1750 CE

C. Western Europe: Spain, England, France, and Holland

1. In western Europe, in contrast to the development of land empires by Russia and China, sea empires were built by Spain, England, France, and Holland (also known as The Netherlands or Dutch) in the Americas.

2. The English, French, and Dutch colonies in the Caribbean and in what would become the United States became part of the mercantile system. Colonies provided raw materials as part of the European powers' goal of global economic strength.

3. France, England, and Holland were also similar to Spain and Portugal with regard to their religious policies in the Americas. They converted natives to Christianity, but were generally less insistent on mass and immediate conversion than the Iberian nations.

Test Tip

Comparisons between the land-based and sea-based empires of this era are common on the AP World History exam.

4. Differences in methods of governance in the Americas developed as well.

   i. Monarchs in Spain and Portugal were more directly involved in governing their colonies than were monarchs in England, France, and the Netherlands.

   ii. Viceroys were like assistant kings over their colonies and reported to the king in many matters. The result was a strict chain of command, with all kinds of matters, important and trivial, being sent to the king for a ruling. Given the huge distance between the Americas and Europe, an answer to a local question could take months.

   iii. The Dutch, French, and British colonies were run differently from those in New Spain or Brazil, with more decision-making on the local level and little micromanagement from Europe.

> Historians say this style of governance is one reason why the British American colonies along the Atlantic coast gradually drew apart from the crown in London. American colonists became used to running their own affairs, fostering a spirit of independence from the crown.

5. In addition to their American empires, Spain and Portugal added territory in the Pacific and Indian Oceans.

   i. The Philippines had been claimed during the explorer Magellan's round-the-world voyage in the early sixteenth century, and Spain was eager to have a base near the riches of China and a population to convert to Christianity.

   ii. Portugal established some outposts along the Atlantic and Indian Ocean coasts of Africa and India, but was not able to achieve sweeping colonization as it had in Brazil.

Test Tip

> *Questions about comparative colonial governments in the Americas are common on the AP World History exam.*

6. Absolute monarchies and a constitutional monarchy in Europe

   i. Other major powers in Europe besides Russia, France, and Spain were under absolute monarchies during this era. In an absolute monarchy, all of the government's power resides in one ruler. It was said that the king was above the law; that is, the law did not necessarily apply to the king. Each king had advisors and a parliament, but all served at the monarch's pleasure.

   ii. England's system was a major exception to this trend. In 1689, its parliament firmly established a constitutional monarchy during the Glorious Revolution. Under that system, the monarch operated under the law and in tandem with the parliament.

      > England's style of constitutional monarchy eventually became the style of government all European kings would accept.

c. 1450–c. 1750 CE

D. The Ottoman Empire

1. The Ottoman Empire reached its peak of power during this era. The empire stretched across North Africa into Southwest Asia and north into modern Turkey, reaching almost to modern Austria.

   i. The Ottomans defeated what was left of the Byzantine Empire when they took Constantinople in 1453, renamed it Istanbul, and continued westward into eastern Europe.

   ii. Geographically and culturally the Ottoman Empire was a link among Europe, Africa, and Asia, encompassing Christian, Jewish, and Muslim faiths.

2. Although the Muslim leaders of the empire did not require Christians and Jews to convert, they did demand that non-Muslim families in the Balkan region of southern Europe hand over young boys to become soldiers for the Turkish army.

   i. These "recruits" were known as *Janissaries* and their "recruitment" was the *devshirme* system.

   ii. Janissaries were trained in Islam and, although they were not Turks, they could rise to prominence in the empire if they showed loyalty and ability—and many did. Sometimes the hope of upward mobility was so strong that Christian parents willingly handed their sons over for Janissary duty.

3. The Ottomans reached the limit of their expansion into Europe when they failed to conquer Vienna, Austria, in the early sixteenth century and again in the late seventeenth century. Like Russia, the Ottoman Empire struggled with its political identity as a part-Asian, part-European empire. Despite its history of battles with Christian Europe, it also sought inclusion in the European diplomatic sphere.

4. The specter of Muslim conquest of all of Europe engulfed many western Christians, especially after the Ottomans conquered Constantinople in 1453.

    i.   This concern for the fate of Christianity was one of the motivations for spreading the faith to the Americas after Columbus's discoveries.

    ii. Another factor was the European fear that trade routes through Constantinople would be cut off by the Ottomans. Thus, the search for alternate routes to the "East" began.

E. Rulers Continued to Use Religion, Art, and Monumental Architecture to Maintain Power

    1. European rulers claimed "divine right," as a source of power, claiming that God had appointed them over their subjects.

    2. The Songhay in West Africa claimed Islam as a major basis of their rule.

    3. The Mughal leaders built impressive mosques and other monumental architecture based on faith (i.e., the Taj Mahal).

    4. Leaders continued to fund art projects such as portraits painted of Qing emperors or works of European Renaissance artists.

II. New Governments in Asia and Europe

As new governments were established by European powers in the Americas, new governments were also established in other areas. Here are three that arose in other regions in the era c. 1450–c. 1750: Tokugawa Japan, Mughal India, and the Netherlands (Holland, the Dutch).

A. Tokugawa Japan

    1. Europeans sailed to Japan in the mid-sixteenth century and took advantage of Japan's feudal system and its lack of a strong central government.

    i.   Portugal sent missionaries and merchants, and was followed by Spain, the Netherlands, and England. They exchanged silver for Japanese manufactured goods.

      ii. At first, the Japanese welcomed the Europeans because they offered improved military and shipbuilding technology, and trade. The Japanese were especially interested in European guns.

      iii. Jesuit missionaries from Portugal had limited success in converting Japanese to Christianity, but one city, Nagasaki, was receptive to the faith and many thousands became Christians.

  2. In the early seventeenth century, the Tokugawa family reunited Japan through military conquests over its rivals.

      i. The leader of the government was the military commander, known as the *Shogun*.

      ii. The Tokugawa Shogunate ruled Japan until the mid-nineteenth century. It considered the influence of outsiders on Japanese culture to be detrimental, so one of the Shogun's first decisions was to run the Europeans out.

      iii. Christians were brutally persecuted and the faith faded in Japan.

      iv. Only one Dutch ship was allowed to trade in one Japanese port once a year. This policy of isolation from Europe lasted until the mid-nineteenth century, when American ships arrived in Edo (Tokyo) Bay to force open Japan's markets.

B. Mughal India

  1. In the early sixteenth century, Muslims from Central Asia, who claimed to be descendents of the Mongol ruler Chinggis Khan, entered South Asia and established the Mughal Empire. ("Mughal" comes from the word "Mongol.") Rare in Indian history, most of South Asia was united under a single government.

  2. Its greatest ruler was Akbar. His greatest legacy was extending religious toleration to the 75 percent of the population that was Hindu.

3. In the beginning of the next era, c. 1750–c. 1900, a new outside invader—the British—arrived and established rule over South Asia, reducing Mughal leaders to ceremonial duties.

4. Like the Ottomans, the Mughals were Muslim rulers of an empire. Unlike the Ottomans, the Mughals' faith was in the minority in their own empire. One of the world's most iconic buildings, the Taj Mahal, was built by a Muslim in the heart of Hindu territory.

C. The Netherlands

1. A small European nation with a global empire, the Netherlands' greatest strength was in the art of the deal. Like the Phoenicians from ancient times, they knew how to get what they wanted, but didn't produce much of their own goods to exchange with others.

2. The Netherlands' economic policies were pro-business, encouraging bank loans, new commercial enterprises, and shipping, with little government interference.

3. The Dutch were perfectly positioned to be a major player in the global economy begun by Portugal and Spain. While the Dutch were slow to "go global"—about one hundred years after their Iberian rivals—once they did, they moved quickly.

   i.   The Dutch sent warships and soldiers under the flag of the Dutch East India Company—also known as the VOC—to take Portuguese outposts in the Indian Ocean region.

   ii. They came to dominate European trade with the "Spice Islands" of present-day Indonesia. "Dutch" chocolate and "java" came from this area.

4. While the Netherlands government's main focus was trade in Southeast Asia, it did own some sugarcane plantations in the Caribbean. The Netherlands also sent colonists to North America, to a place they called New Netherlands, with its main outpost of New Amsterdam on Manhattan Island. In the 1660s, the British took New Amsterdam and renamed it New York.

c. 1450–c. 1750 ce

III. **The Collapse of Empires**

A. Aztec

1. In fourteenth-century Mesoamerica, a new empire arose, the Aztec. You have learned about their capital, Tenochtitlán, situated in the middle of Lake Texcoco, and about their unique farming method of floating human-made islands.

2. The Aztec Empire expanded through conquest and demanded tribute from the vanquished people.

    i. Little effort was made to assimilate the conquered groups into the empire as long as tribute and trade goods flowed into the Aztec treasury.

    ii. Trade was an important part of Aztec society, with precious metals, feathers, food, and people for sale in large marketplaces.

3. Aztec rulers claimed to be descended from the gods, so government and religion intertwined closely, not unlike in ancient Egypt.

    i. Human sacrifice was a vital part of the Aztec faith. The belief was that the gods needed human blood to ensure that the sun rose every day.

    ii. Slaves and captured enemy warriors were frequently offered up in these blood sacrifices, creating the never-ending need for human subjects.

4. By the early sixteenth century, the Aztecs faced internal pressures due to unrest stirring among the conquered people of the empire, who were increasingly angry about the high degree of tribute that in turn caused them economic hardship.

5. At the same time, outside pressure was forcefully applied with the arrival of Spanish conquistadors and their superior weapons and desire for gold. The Aztec empire crumbled astonishingly fast.

B. Inca

1. The largest empire of the Americas before the arrival of the Europeans was governed by the Inca from their capital Cuzco, in the Andes Mountains.

    i. Lasting for only about one hundred years, from the mid-fifteenth century to the mid-sixteenth century, the Inca Empire stretched along most of the Pacific coast of South America.

    ii. Like the Aztecs, the Inca expanded their empire through military conquest and the tribute they demanded from the people they defeated. They, too, had an emperor who claimed to be descended from the gods.

    iii. Unlike the Aztecs, the Inca incorporated the vanquished into the empire, requiring, for example, that the defeated people learn the Incan language.

2. Under the Incan system, all land, food, and manufactured products were owned by the government.

    i. The Inca people were required to contribute a portion of their goods to the government for redistribution by the large Inca bureaucracy. Historians refer to this as "Inca socialism."

3. One of the most interesting features of Incan civilization was their record-keeping system on knotted strings, known as *quipu.* The accounting system, kept by the government bureaucracy, was based on the number and position of knots and the color of the strings in the cords.

4. Like the Aztecs, the Inca were also facing internal strife when the Spanish arrived in the 1530s.

    i. A civil war for control of the throne was raging and at about the same time smallpox began to decimate the population. These stresses made the empire susceptible to outside invasion, and it came in the form of less than 200 well-armed conquistadors.

    ii. The emperor was killed and the age of the Inca Empire was over.

C. Byzantine

1. After centuries of warfare with Muslim forces, the Byzantine Empire had been reduced to only the great cultural and trading center of Constantinople. In 1453, its defenders succumbed to superior forces from the Ottoman Empire, ending a civilization that had existed on its own since the fall of Rome in 476 CE, and as part of the Roman Empire for almost half a millennium before that.

2. The greatest symbol of the transfer of power from the Christians to the Muslims in Constantinople/Istanbul was the Hagia Sophia, an Eastern Orthodox Christian Church, which was converted into a mosque.

Test Tip

The Hagia Sophia's blending of Greek Orthodox and Islamic architecture is an example of the kind of cultural borrowing that AP World History test developers get excited about.

PERIOD 5

INDUSTRIALIZATION AND GLOBAL INTEGRATION

c. 1750–c. 1900 CE

Industrialization
and Its Effects
c. 1750–c. 1900 CE

In the fifth period in AP World History, c. 1750–c. 1900, the greatest revolution since the Neolithic era (c. 8000 BCE) occurred: the Industrial Revolution. It fundamentally changed the human experience and continues to affect the world today. Although some people in the early twenty-first century have not experienced industrialization directly, only a miniscule number have not been affected by it.

The Industrial Revolution changed governments, family life, global and local economies, food production, migration, war, art and literature, the environment, transportation, communication, population growth, and rural and urban areas. It led to the Age of Imperialism, political revolutions, communism, World War I, women's rights, multinational corporations, and the "traditional" Western family.

I. Causes of the Industrial Revolution

A. The Industrial Revolution Began in Western Europe, Specifically in Britain.

1. Western Europe's government policies

   As western Europe built political and economic empires in the New World, the flow of silver and gold from the New World into Europe's treasuries made their societies the richest in the world.

   i. European governments—especially Britain—invested part of this income in the form of monetary prizes to individuals who invented more efficient ways to transport goods, grow crops, defeat enemies—anything that might significantly contribute to the nation's increased share of the global mercantilist pie.

2. Geography

   i.   Incentives like government-sponsored prizes for useful inventions were factors that triggered the Industrial Revolution. Another factor was the right type of natural resources to create the inventions.

   ii.   Britain had coal and iron, good soil, fast-moving rivers to turn waterwheels that powered machines, and many natural harbors to import raw materials from far-away colonies.

   iii.   Products manufactured from those raw materials were exported back to millions of colonial consumers and other markets around the globe.

   iv.   Belgium, Germany, and France had similar favorable geographic conditions and were quick to follow Britain's lead in developing industry.

3. Economic and social mobility

   i.   Especially in Britain, and to a lesser degree in the rest of western Europe, people could move up the economic and social ladder if they developed a money-making invention. This incentive spurred Britain to become "a nation of tinkerers," as one observer put it.

   ii.   Banks loaned money to inventors in whom they had faith. As noted above, European governments offered prizes for inventions that they considered helpful to their global economic and political goals. These conditions did not exist outside Europe at the beginning of this era.

4. Workforce

   i.   Britain had a large number of people skilled in working with metal tools. Those skills were necessary for the creation of the machines that would be used to develop industry.

ii. Many agricultural workers in Britain were forced off farmland by a government-approved policy called the enclosure movement. The landless peasants migrated to cities, forming a large potential workforce for factories.

5. Why didn't the Industrial Revolution begin somewhere else?

   i. Africa had a great deal more natural resources than did western Europe; Ming China had a well-organized government and a very strong economy; and India and China had a tradition of technological development.

   ii. Only western Europe, however, had all the necessary factors for industrial development by the mid-eighteenth century: incentive, materials, and skilled-labor.

II. Beginnings of the Industrial Revolution

A. Mechanization of Textile Production

1. British inventors developed machines that could mass-produce cloth and thread.

2. These muscle-powered, wood-and-iron machines were a hit with manufacturers because they cranked out cloth faster and cheaper than hand-making methods.

3. Bigger and quicker machines were developed, and they were massed into large buildings called factories. Waterwheels turning in fast-moving streams provided power for the machines.

B. The Steam Engine

1. By the 1760s, inventors in Britain had developed the steam engine—one of the most revolutionary inventions of all time—and made waterpower obsolete.

   i. With the development of the steam engine, factories didn't have to be built next to a stream—they could be anywhere.

   ii. Connecting cloth- and thread-making machines to steam engines increased production many times beyond what humans could do. Mass production of goods made machine-made clothing affordable to just about everyone in European society.

2. Technological changes cascaded quickly after the introduction of the steam engine.

   i.   The successes of machine-produced cloth and thread led to the invention of the cotton gin, a machine that took seeds out of cotton to prepare it for thread and cloth manufacturing.

   ii. The cotton gin operated many times faster than any human and when it was hooked up to a steam engine, it operated even faster.

3. Two early nineteenth-century inventions involving the steam engine drastically altered transportation.

   i.   In the United States, the first steamboat made seven thousand years of sail power obsolete.

   ii. In Britain, the steam-powered locomotive marked the beginning of the end of the age of the horse in modern societies.

 III. **The Industrial Revolution Motors On**

A. Fossil Fuels

1. Coal was the initial fuel for the steam engines of the Industrial Revolution, but as the nineteenth century progressed, petroleum was increasingly used, especially after the development of the internal combustion (diesel and later, gasoline) engine. Both provided vastly greater amounts of energy than any previous form of power.

B. Steel

1. Advancements in steel production led to mass production of this alloy that was stronger, lighter, and more flexible than iron.

    i.   Steel factories centered in regions near iron and coal mines, materials vital to steel production.

    ii. Western Europe again led the way, followed soon by the United States, Japan, and Russia. Steel became the "king of metals" in the Industrial Age.

C. Industrialization Spreads

1. The United States

    i.   The United States was quick to follow Britain's lead in industrialization. The cotton gin, invented in Connecticut in the late eighteenth century, made cotton production highly profitable.

    ii. In the South, single-crop cotton plantations boomed, as did slavery.

    iii. British-style factories that turned American cotton into textiles popped up in the Northeast. The South produced so much cotton that much of it was shipped to England's factories.

    iv. Railroads sprang up in the Northeast first and soon connected to farming areas in the Midwest and South, speeding up delivery of crops and farm animals to processing factories in Chicago and other cities in the North.

    v. By 1900, the United States was the world's biggest steel producer and U.S. Steel Corporation was the world's first billion-dollar corporation.

2. Japan

    i.   Using a show of industrial force, the U.S. government sent navy ships to force open the trade door with Japan in the 1850s. The Japanese government responded, not by resisting, but by transforming its government, society, and industry.

    ii. In their program of Western-style industrialization, the Japanese built factories that specialized in silk textiles.

c. 1750–c. 1900 CE

      iii. One significant difference between Japanese and Western industrialization was that the Japanese government had close ties to factory corporations. The government often built factories, then sold them to investors but stayed actively involved in their finances and business decisions.

3. Russia

      i. Unlike Japan and the "West," Russia's industrial progress was limited in this era.

      ii. The government's primary focus was on supporting the elite owners of large agricultural estates. Serfdom was still in place until the mid-nineteenth century. The government freed the serfs, but unlike the United States and Japan, Russia was slow to shift to industrialization.

      iii. Late in this era, the Russian government sought foreign investment in its industrial program. Russia became a top producer of steel and built the Trans-Siberian Railway, passing the United States in having the world's longest railroad.

      iv. Despite these accomplishments, Russia's economy remained largely mired in the fifteenth century. Peasant laborers grew mostly wheat and potatoes for export from the large estates still owned by friends of the czar.

4. Latin America

      i. Europeans invested great amounts of money to jump-start industrialization in Latin America.

      ii. Great expectations followed and some railroad routes were built, but overall, like Russia, Latin America remained largely an exporter of crops grown by peasant labor.

      iii. Products included coffee, bananas, wheat, beef, and sugar. Industrialized nations sought copper, a major export of Mexico.

5. India

      i. England established its rule (*raj*) over India near the beginning of the era c. 1750–c.1900.

ii.   India was a leading grower of cotton, and England eagerly imported the fabric for its textile mills. Toward the end of this era, under British authority, Indian textile factories began to produce machine-made cotton thread and cloth, and the production of hand-made textiles began to decline.

iii. India's age of rapid industrial growth, however, waited until the late twentieth century.

6. Industrialization in other regions

   i.   Like the Russians, the Ottoman Empire had limited progress in developing modern industry in this era. The empire's leaders failed to recognize the degree to which the Industrial Revolution was increasing the West's political, economic, and military power. Unlike Japan's leaders at this time, the Ottomans were divided over following western Europe's industrial model.

   ii. Africa remained a provider of natural resources to the world's industrial giants. The greatest export in terms of cost was diamonds and gold from South Africa. In the Age of Imperialism, Europe's governments and businesses preferred to keep its African colonies dependent on them.

   iii. China rejected most things Western in this era and remained largely out of the production end of the Industrial Revolution. Some foreign investment provided for railroads and steamships, but overall the Middle Kingdom stuck with human labor to produce crops and hand-made items for export.

     ➤ The new industrial powers in western Europe, the United States, Russia, and Japan took advantage of China's weak government by forcing open exclusive trade regions—spheres of influence—in China. So Russia traded in one region of China, Britain in another, and France in yet another.

     ➤ At the end of this era, these nations accepted a U.S. proposal for an "open door policy" in China, ending the spheres of influence and allowing open access to all of China's markets.

Test Tip

Questions comparing industrialization in the West, Russia, and/or Japan have appeared on every AP World History exam since it was first administered.

IV. **Social Effects of the Industrial Revolution**

A. Western Europe and the United States

1. In these "Western" regions, the rapid changes that industrialization had on the economy affected everyday life. England was the first to experience these changes.

   i. The factory system demanded a great deal of labor, so families moved from farms to cities to work in textile and other kinds of factories.

   ii. Another factor in the move from farms to cities was the loss of farm jobs due to the increased use of labor-saving devices in agriculture.

2. Over time, wages went up so much that working outside the home became primarily a "man's job."

   i. As factories became more efficient, less human labor was required, so, for the most part, women and children left factory work.

   ii. In many areas of the West, however, children continued to be employed in coal mines and in agricultural labor.

3. As steady wages increased over time, a new social class arose in the industrial West: the middle class. This economic and social group between the rich and the poor had always existed, but in this era, it exploded in size and political power.

4. Women were expected to marry and stay home to take care of their husbands and children, creating the traditional family structure in the West.

     i.   Urban families had fewer children than their rural counterparts.

     ii.   Single women increasingly found employment as teachers, replacing men in these jobs.

5. As the twentieth century approached, women began to replace men in the business environment as secretaries and telephone operators.

     i.   Women were not allowed to vote in most Western societies until after World War I.

     ii.   Fewer children were needed for factory work, and governments in the West, concerned about the prospect of millions of unsupervised children running around with nothing to do, passed laws requiring school attendance.

6. The Industrial Revolution caused more cities to develop and rise to unprecedented sizes. Seeking a steady income, people left farm life and moved to cities to work in industrial jobs.

     i.   With the boom in urban population came overcrowded living conditions, high levels of pollution, higher crime rates, and a poor and increasingly discontent working class.

     ii.   Pressures from these conditions led to proposals for sweeping changes in government policies in Europe and the United States.

7. Art and literature

     i.   Looking at the gritty life of the overcrowded industrial cities, artists abandoned the optimism of the Romantic school of art and shifted to Realism, painting dark scenes of city life, exemplified by locomotives belching black smoke.

     ii.   The camera was invented, which artists feared would put them out of business. The artistic style called *Impressionism* was in direct contrast to photography's graphic realism. Artists painted deliberately unfocused scenes of nature—their "impression" of the scene. French artists led the way in this school of art.

iii. Writers also responded to the effects of the Industrial Revolution. Charles Dickens wrote stories about life among the struggling urban laboring classes in soot-covered London in the early nineteenth century in his classics, *A Christmas Carol* and *Oliver Twist*, among others.

The AP World History exam focuses most often on the effects of industrialization on Japanese society. Be sure you know about the conditions endured by young women who were sent from rural areas by their families to work in silk factories. Unhealthy working conditions and threats from male supervisors were the subject of songs and poems written by so-called factory girls.

B. Latin America

1. The limited impact of the Industrial Revolution on Latin America meant that continuities in social structures and gender roles remained through this era.

2. In another major social development, millions of Europeans migrated to Latin America in the nineteenth century seeking new economic opportunities.

3. In an interesting parallel, thousands of Japanese immigrants poured into the west coast of South America, mostly to work as laborers.

V. Multinational Corporations

A. With the ever-expanding global market for machine-made goods came businesses that operated on a global scale. You have read of banks that loaned money for foreign investments and of the British East India and Dutch East India companies—two of the world's first multinational businesses.

B. Another business that operated on an international scale was the U.S.-based United Fruit Company. It owned huge tracts of banana plantations throughout Central America. The produce was shipped to the United States and Europe.

C. The exchange of goods and money among the industrialized economies grew so fast that they established a gold standard for world currencies. An agreed-upon international price of gold became the measure by which nations determined the relative value of their money systems.

Test Tip

The growth of multinational—or transnational—corporations is a frequent topic on the AP World History exam.

VI. **The "Second Industrial Revolution"**

A. From Steam to Gas

1. In the second half of the nineteenth century, the pace of industrialization quickened and so did the number of inventions. Historians call this a "Second Industrial Revolution."

2. Instead of focusing on textile production and steam power, the second industrial revolution ran on the internal combustion (gasoline or diesel) engine.

3. It also differed from the initial Industrial Revolution because there were more inventions related to electrical systems, scientific discoveries, and medicine. All had applications for the mechanization of warfare.

B. Communication

1. The first major development in the area of communication was the U.S. invention of the telegraph in the 1840s.

   i. By the late 1850s, a telegraph cable had been extended under the Atlantic Ocean, linking the British Isles to Canada and the United States.

   ii. By the 1870s, communication across the Pacific was achieved, and by 1902, the entire global British Empire was connected by telegraph.

c. 1750–c. 1900 CE

2. In 1876, the telephone was invented in the United States. Its popularity was different from the telegraph in that the user needed no special training, making it a home-use product.

3. The radio (or "wireless telegraph") was in its developmental stage near the end of this era.

C. Transportation

1. After the development of the steamboat and the steam locomotive, the next major step in transportation was the electric trolley car and the subterranean transportation system, or the subway. Both were mass-transit systems, first used in large cities like London, Paris, and New York.

2. The automobile was invented in Germany in the 1880s. In this era, it was mostly an experimental device and an object of curiosity.

D. Science and Medicine

1. The modern science of chemistry began in the era c.1750–c.1900.

   i. Systematic studies of chemical compounds and the composition of different forms of matter gave scientists insights into how nature works.

   ii. Toward the end of the era, scientists were developing chemical compounds in the lab—some were powerful fertilizers that were used to grow crops (and thus more food) more efficiently than before.

2. Advances in medicine in this era included smallpox and rabies vaccinations, sterilization of surgical instruments, the use of anesthetics during surgery, and aspirin, to name a few. Governments oversaw programs that provided clean drinking water in cities. These and many other examples led to healthier, longer lives in the industrialized world.

3. Science and faith crossed swords in the person of Charles Darwin.

   i. His investigations of animals of the South Pacific led him to conclude that natural selection, not God, determined the viability of species on Earth. He also theorized that humans and apes had similar characteristics and must therefore have common ancestors.

ii. These pronouncements began furious debates about the nature of humanity and its place among animals in the world. His ideas about survival of the fittest in the animal kingdoms led some Europeans to transfer the concept to human civilizations.

iii. *Social Darwinism*—wherein the superior races must naturally defeat inferior ones—had enormous implications in the upcoming Age of Imperialism.

Western Imperialism
c. 1750–c. 1900 CE

Imperial means "empire," and in the era c. 1750–c. 1900, the western European powers—and to a lesser extent the United States and Japan—established empires outside their borders. Western Europe's empires were global, with territories in Africa, Asia, North and South America, Australia, and islands in the Pacific, Atlantic, and Indian Oceans. Britain's territories were so vast, British subjects could claim, "The sun never sets on the British Empire." By the end of this era, Britain's imperial possessions covered one-fourth of the Earth.

In the first era of European imperialism in the sixteenth and seventeenth centuries, the focus was on the Americas. In the late eighteenth and through the nineteenth centuries, the nations of Europe restarted the process, but this time Africa and Asia were the primary targets. Ironically, during this age of "new" imperialism, Spain and Portugal, two of the greatest empires of the previous era, began to decline in global power.

I. **Industrialized Nations Accumulate Colonies Around the Globe**

A. Causes of Imperialism

   1. The Industrial Revolution

      i. Using inventions of the Industrial Revolution such as steamboats, railroads, and machine guns, western European nations were able to overwhelm Africans with the new technologies. As a result, large numbers of Europeans with superior military forces reached the interior of Africa for the first time.

2. Nationalism

   i. Nationalism—a sense of pride and devotion to one's country—was a powerful force in Europe and the Americas in the early nineteenth century. It was an important factor in empire-building in this era.

   ii. National pride showed itself in two ways. First, the older European nations engaged in an unofficial competition to see who could grab the most territory around the world. It was a kind of "keeping up with the Joneses" rivalry. If England claimed *this*, then France wanted *that*, and on it went. Second, new nations, such as Germany and Italy, wanted to show that they belonged with the so-called Great Powers, so they got into the imperialism game, too.

Test Tip

Be sure to study maps of imperialism in Africa and Asia c. 1914. There will be at least one or two questions on the AP World History exam related to imperialism.

3. Economics

   i. Controlling world markets was an idea going back to the first round of European imperialism in the sixteenth and seventeenth centuries. In this "new" imperialism, not only were governments and their treasuries involved, but also multinational corporations.

   ii. These multinational corporations put pressure on governments to help them claim their "share" of the global economy. The economic stakes were greater because the amount and value of global trade was also greater. Africa and Asia held vast amounts of raw materials, such as cotton, rubber, and minerals that industrialized nations wanted to keep their economies booming.

   iii. European imperialists saw Africa and Asia as potential markets for their mass-produced goods, such as cloth and steel.

4. "The White Man's Burden"

   i. The white Europeans believed they were doing their "little brown brothers" in Africa, Asia, and Oceania a favor by conquering them. After all, they reasoned, the Europeans developed the inventions of the Industrial Revolution that made it possible to travel around the world. To many Europeans, bringing "them" technology, plus education, medicine, and Christianity, was a noble cause.

   ii. The English writer Rudyard Kipling wrote a poem entitled "The White Man's Burden" about these ideas.

B. Imperialism in Africa

1. European imperialism in Africa before the nineteenth century

   i. Even though Europeans had shared much history with the people of Africa's Mediterranean coast going back to the Classical Era (c. 600 BCE–c. 600 CE), they lacked the ability to move south of the Sahara Desert into Africa's interior.

   ii. In the sixteenth century, the Portuguese set up some military outposts around South Africa's Cape of Good Hope and along the rim of the Indian Ocean, but they did not establish any colonies. Within a hundred years, Europeans were transporting slaves from the Atlantic coast of Africa to the Americas but, again, did not attempt to establish colonies along West Africa's coast.

   iii. The Dutch East India Company (the "VOC") established a colony at Cape Town, South Africa, in the mid-seventeenth century, and over the next one hundred years, Dutch settlers established farms throughout the region.

2. At the beginning of the nineteenth century, Britain began sending settlers into South Africa, and these British settlers eventually experienced strife with the Dutch colonists ("Boers")—not to mention heightening tensions that

already existed between the Dutch and the African people of the region.

3. Starting in the 1830s, France followed Britain's example and became a major African colonial power, first in Algeria and then across most of northwest Africa.

4. Belgium began the infamous "scramble for Africa" in the 1880s when it grabbed an enormous area in the "heart" of Africa—The Congo. When the other European powers saw Belgium become a major colonial power, they began a rush to outdo each other in gaining territories. The "Great Powers" of Europe met at the Berlin Conference of 1884–1885 to divide Africa among themselves peacefully. They didn't invite anyone *from* Africa, however, to participate in the division of these lands. Clearly, this approach would lead to problems.

5. By 1914, the sweep of European colonialism was so complete that only two areas in Africa were independent nations: Ethiopia (Italy tried, but failed, to make it a colony) and Liberia (founded as a colony for former U.S. slaves).

C. Imperialism in Asia and the Pacific

1. In contrast to their experiences in Africa, Europeans found that much of Asia could not be brought into their empires because Asian governments were strong enough to keep the Europeans at bay—the Ottoman Empire still had a formidable military force, Japan was becoming one of the major powers, and Europeans desired China's economic assets more than its land.

2. The biggest example of European imperialism in Asia was India. It was England's "jewel in the crown" of colonies.

   i. After England won the Seven Years' War against France in 1763, France lost control of most of its North American and South Asian holdings. The English took possession of Canada and the eastern half of what was to become the United States. With significant help from the British East India Company (EIC), they established rule over South Asia.

ii. By the mid-nineteenth century, the EIC had folded, and the British government began direct control over its colony in South Asia and remained the colonial power there until 1947. The British called their rule in India the *raj*, and Queen Victoria was named empress of India. In addition, during the nineteenth century, the British extended colonial control to Malaysia and Singapore and several islands in the Pacific and Indian oceans. They used these islands as strategic refueling stations for their steam-powered military and cargo ships.

D. The United States, Germany, and Japan Build Empires

1. U.S. Imperialism

i. The U.S. government believed that it was destined to rule the North American continent "from sea to shining sea."

➤ In the 1840s, victory in a war with Mexico yielded Texas and all the land to the Pacific coast south of Canada.

➤ By the end of the century, along with the other imperial powers, the United States began acquiring islands in the Pacific for strategic refueling bases.

➤ Spain's decline as a world power was sealed when it lost the Spanish-American War (1898–1901). As a result of its victory in this war, the United States added the Philippines, Guam, and Puerto Rico to its colonial holdings.

➤ Finally, the United States annexed Hawaii, with its rich sugar plantations and vital port, Pearl Harbor.

2. German Imperialism

i. Germany, of course, is in Europe, but because it was established only in the late nineteenth century, it merits separate discussion. The German Empire was founded in 1871. Its leaders were determined to make their new nation a formidable power in Europe.

c. 1750–c. 1900 CE

     ii. In that era, international respect was granted to those with the most "toys," meaning colonies. At the Berlin Conference, Germany wrangled several African territories in strategic moves to counter British gains in Africa. They also claimed parts of the Marshall, Solomon, and Caroline Islands, and Western Samoa, which were all in the South Pacific.

  3. Japanese Imperialism

     i. When Japan changed its government in the 1860s in the Meiji Restoration, it was eager to join Germany and the United States in establishing a place with the major powers of Europe.

     ii. Japan began an aggressive campaign to create an empire in the Pacific region. Japan also wanted to counter Russian gains in East Asia after that nation completed the Trans-Siberian Railway.

     iii. An early test of Japan's new "Western-style" army was in the Sino-Japanese war with China in the 1890s. Japan claimed Korea after their victory in that war. Everyone, except Japan, was shocked when the Japanese defeated Russia in the Russo-Japanese War in 1905. The conflict was for control of territories in Manchuria and, again, Korea.

II. Results of Western Imperialism

A. Africa

  1. Europeans peacefully divided Africa among themselves at the Berlin Conference in 1885, paying little attention to the concerns of the African people who were affected.

     i. Europe's confidence in its racial and cultural superiority did not leave much room for debate about the potential disadvantages of imperialism.

     ii. Social Darwinism—the idea that civilizations with superior technology and tactics *deserved* to conquer those without these advantages—was a powerful force in this era.

2. At Berlin, the British attempted to form a series of colonies that stretched "from Cape Town to Cairo," that is, from South Africa to Egypt. They were stymied by Germany, who inserted a colony in East Africa.

   i. The best-known imperialist in this era was Cecil Rhodes, the British entrepreneur whose business was in the gold and diamond mines of South Africa. The colony of Rhodesia was named after him.

3. Europeans created "White dominions" and "settler colonies."

   i. Britain developed "White dominions," places where the colonists, through disease and conquest, eventually outnumbered the native people.

      ➤ "White dominions" occurred in Oceania (Australia and New Zealand) and in North America (in their American and Canadian colonies).

   ii. "Settler colonies" were areas where Europeans settled and ruled, but remained a minority.

      ➤ South Africa and Singapore were two British examples of settler colonies.

      ➤ The Philippines was a settler colony for the United States.

      ➤ A French example of a settler colony was Algeria in North Africa, where over 100,000 European colonists claimed rule over an Arab Muslim population of more than 2 million.

4. Social efforts by imperialists had mixed results.

   i. Christian missionaries had success spreading their faith in sub-Saharan Africa, but they made no progress in the Muslim north.

      ➤ Europeans were determined to "civilize" their "little brown brothers" by dressing them in Western fashions and teaching them Western

c. 1750–c. 1900 CE

behavior, which usually only confused the local people.

    ii.   Some African elites were sent to European schools in an attempt to bring them over to pro-Western thinking. These efforts often had unintended consequences for the colonizers, as you will see.

  5. Popular European literature with imperialist themes set in Africa included *Tarzan*, the story of an English boy raised by apes in the African jungle, and *Heart of Darkness*, a novel that criticized imperialist attitudes toward Africans.

B. Asia and the Pacific

  1. Europeans had much more contact with Asia before the "new imperialism" of this era, so the impact of their efforts was minimized in most areas.

    i.   Unlike their approach in Africa, the Europeans used a variety of methods to obtain direct and indirect control in Asia.

       ➤ In Malaysia, for example, the British made treaties with local rulers that resulted in indirect control of that vital trade region.

       ➤ France used a combination of military force and diplomacy to bring the Southeast Asia territory of Indochina into its empire.

  2. Once England established itself in India, it primarily used "native" Indian forces to maintain British authority. These *Sepoys* were generally loyal to the crown, but you will learn about an important departure from that trend below. The British exported cotton and tea from its Indian colonies.

  3. The most infamous example of European imperialism in Asia was the opium wars with China in the mid-nineteenth century.

    i.   To offset huge trade deficits, the British began smuggling opium into China's ports, in defiance of Chinese laws. China's diplomatic protests went unheeded, and the Opium Wars broke out between the two nations. Britain easily won these wars.

ii. China was forced into a series of Unequal Treaties that increased Britain's economic presence and handed the island of Hong Kong to British authority.

iii. Other nations, including Russia, Japan, France, and Germany, jumped at the chance to make their own unequal treaties with China. Rather than attempt political colonization of China, these nations created "spheres of influence" within China, with each foreign nation having exclusive trading rights in "its" portion of China.

iv. As noted in Chapter 13, the United States proposed a trading free-for-all in China, called the *open door policy*, which was accepted by the nations involved. China's opinion didn't count.

4. European attempts to bring Christianity to Asia in this era met with fewer converts than in Africa. However, in China as many as 100,000 people joined the Christian faith.

5. In popular European culture, books aimed at younger people highlighted these "exotic" lands and were especially nationalistic, praising the Europeans' dedication to the "white man's burden." *The Jungle Book*, about a young Indian boy's adventures in South Asia, was one famous title.

III. Local Reactions to Imperialism

A. Africa

1. Reactions of Africans to European imperialism ranged from warfare to reluctant acceptance to full cooperation.

i. The French spent years in northwest Africa subduing local rebellions.

c. 1750–c. 1900 CE

ii. At the end of the nineteenth century, descendants of Dutch settlers believed that the newly arrived British were violating their property rights to land and slaves. In addition, they were angry about the gold and diamonds the British were hauling out of the territory once claimed by Boers.

iii. The British battled Zulus and Dutch Boers in southern Africa, and Muslims in Sudan. The Boer war left hundreds of thousands of casualties in its wake.

2. Other Africans signed treaties and acted as guides and interpreters for Europeans. Still others cooperated fully with the European powers. Often these were members of the African ruling elite families, who benefited financially and materially from working closely with the outsiders. Some were sent to Europe for full indoctrination into Western culture. After returning to their homelands, many of these elites began preparing independence movements.

B. Asia

1. In Asia, the same pattern emerged as in Africa: Some local people rebelled violently, while others tried to "fit in" with the colonial powers' ways of life.

   i. Military resistance to European occupation occurred in Afghanistan (against the British), the Philippines (against the United States), and in China (against foreigners in general).

      ➤ The Taiping and Boxer rebellions in China were highly anti-foreign in their nature.

      ➤ In India, the "native" army, whose soldiers were employed by the British colonial government and the East India Company, rebelled. It took British forces a year to suppress the rebellion. This resulted in the end of the Mughal Dynasty, which had begun in India in the sixteenth century, the dissolution of the East India Company, and the beginnings of the British *raj* over India.

2. There were also examples of cooperation. Many Indian soldiers remained loyal to the British in the Sepoy rebellion. The king of Siam (Thailand) decided to proactively deflect European colonization by inviting British representatives to help "westernize" his country.

The AP World History exam has frequently asked questions related to African and Asian responses to European imperialism.

C. 1750–C. 1900 CE

Nationalism, Revolution, and Reform

c. 1750–c. 1900 CE

The Industrial Revolution was not the only kind of revolution in this era. There were many political revolutions around the globe, but particularly on both sides of the Atlantic.

Ideas from the European Enlightenment movement sparked revolutions based on concepts of liberty and equality. New nations were formed and older governments instituted reforms from 1750 to 1900. *Nationalism*, a sense of strong identity with others who share a common history, religion, and/or language, led many people to create and live in new nations.

The *Enlightenment* was an era of new ideas in Western thought about science, religion, art, government, and philosophy. The movement peaked in the eighteenth century in Europe, but because Europe's culture spread globally during the Age of Imperialism, Enlightenment ideas did too.

I. **Ideas from Europe's Enlightenment Era Spark Changes in Governments**

A. Enlightenment Ideas

Ideas from the Scientific Revolution (see Chapter 11) sparked the belief among European intellectuals that the human condition could be explained and improved if rational thought were applied to everyday life.

1. Individual equality

   i. Enlightenment thinkers (*philosophes*—French for "philosophers"), such as the French writers Voltaire and

Rousseau, wrote that all men were created equal—that no person deserved extra privileges over others just for being born. A king was not automatically "better" than a commoner. The ideas in the U.S. Declaration of Independence reflect this belief.

2. Individual liberty

   i. This Enlightenment ideal is that people should be free to make their own personal and economic decisions in life. Slavery should be abolished. Freedom of speech and religion were "natural rights."

3. Limited governments

   i. Enlightenment thinkers Locke and Rousseau wrote that governments and the people had a "social contract" between them. If the leader of the government failed to serve the people well, the people had a right to revolt.

   ii. The favorite form of government of Enlightenment thinkers was a republic—a constitution, an elected legislature of representatives, and no king.

   iii. In addition, Adam Smith insisted that governments end their mercantilism policies and stay out of the way of the "natural" cycles of the economy.

B. Political Revolutions in the Atlantic World

1. American Revolution

   i. The first place Enlightenment ideas were tried on a large scale was in the English American colonies. You know the story, but in the context of world history, the effects of the American Revolution were enormous. The idea that a group of colonies could overthrow their "oppressors" and establish—on purpose, no less—a representative government based on the Enlightenment principles inspired revolutions around the world into the twenty-first century.

2. French Revolution

   i. Soon afterward, the French revolted against their king, but in contrast to the American Revolution, the struggle was not a colonial one. In the spirit of Enlightenment ideas, the slogan of the French Revolution was "Liberty, equality, fraternity (brotherhood)." The French Revolution expressed its roots in the Enlightenment in the *Declaration of the Rights of Man and of the Citizen*.

ii. After attempting a constitutional monarchy like Britain's, and after the French king was executed, a republic was established. Another contrast with the American Revolution was the amount of blood that accompanied the French Revolution. As many as 30,000 people lost their lives to overenthusiastic revolutionary leaders, who were in turn executed and replaced by a military dictator who restored order, Napoleon Bonaparte.

iii. Napoleon claimed to be a child of the Enlightenment, and he did enact reforms such as equality before the law, but he was no fan of republics. After Napoleon's defeat by a coalition of other European nations, including Britain and Russia, the Congress of Vienna reorganized Europe's boundaries to include several new nations. You will learn about the results of the decisions of the Congress of Vienna later in this chapter.

C. Haiti and Latin America

1. Haiti

i. The French Revolution's first "child" was delivered in the early nineteenth century in its colony of Haiti, then known as Saint Domingue. The vast majority of the residents were slaves. Led by Toussaint Louverture, they revolted against their white French masters. Napoleon sent an army to the rebellion, but it was defeated.

ii. The result of this first successful slave revolt was the establishment of the second republic in the New World, after the United States. In its revolution, Haiti's rich plantation economy of large exportable crops of sugar and coffee was destroyed and was replaced by small farms that exported very little.

Be sure to know the similarities and differences among the Haitian, French, and Russian (see Chapter 18) revolutions for the AP World History exam.

2. Latin America

   i. By 1830, the success of the Haitian revolution inspired the rest of Latin America's colonies to rise up against Spanish and Portuguese rule.

   ii. Led by upper-class Creole elites—the most famous was Simón Bolívar—one by one, the colonies gained independence through military victories against the colonizers, hastening the decline of Spain as a world power.

   iii. Unlike the United States, which had a sizable educated middle class, Latin American countries had an enormous social and economic chasm between the few elite and the many poor.

   iv. Similar to the U.S. experience, the elite remained in power when the revolutions were over. Establishing stable governments was a common difficulty in the new Latin American nations, including Mexico and Brazil. There was also a lack of significant social and economic change for the non-elites.

   v. Although women's rights were frequently discussed by the European philosophes, in Latin America and elsewhere, they were largely set aside until the twentieth century.

II. The Effects of the Industrial Revolution—Revolts, Reforms, and Famine

Napoleon's wars across western Europe and into Russia resulted in a redrawing of the map of Europe after his defeat in the early nineteenth century. Nations created by the Congress of Vienna were often drawn with little attention to the desires of the people in those new nations. Huge changes in society from the Industrial Revolution resulted in unrest among the urban poor. Revolts from the 1820s through the 1840s in Europe had two major goals: political freedom and economic opportunity.

A. Pressures in Cities and Factories

1. Overcrowded cities created many problems, including scarce housing, disease, and unemployment.

   i. The lower classes suffered the most, and discontent spilled into the streets of many major European cities. Government leaders were often slow to respond to the calls for reform because they were either overwhelmed by, or did not care about, the numerous problems facing societies in the early years of the Industrial Revolution.

   ii. By the mid-nineteenth century, however, political pressure from the increasingly important middle class stirred governments in western and central Europe to begin providing assistance to the urban working classes.

2. Poor working conditions in factories, including hazardous machinery, long hours, and low pay, led to anger and resentment among the laboring classes.

B. Calls for Change

1. From the 1820s through the 1840s, European activists rallied the urban poor to take to the streets. Members of the middle class were urged to use their new voting power to call for political rights for working-class men, increased pay, and safer working conditions in factories.

   i. Only a few men and women lobbied for voting rights for women in the late eighteenth and early nineteenth centuries. Mary Wollstonecraft, a British writer, penned *A Vindication of the Rights of Women* and France's Olympe de Gouges wrote the *Declaration of the Rights of Women and the Female Citizen*, each calling for equality.

c. 1750–c. 1900 CE

ii. Labor unions, representing the collective power of many workers, began to form. The labor unions were illegal in most western European nations until later in the nineteenth century.

2. Karl Marx was considered the most radical activist among those calling for political change.

i. In 1848, commenting on the plight of the working poor in London, Marx's "Communist Manifesto" demanded overthrow of the "haves" ("bourgeoisie") by the "have-nots" ("proletariat").

ii. He envisioned the creation of a classless society where all people were politically, socially, and economically equal. At the time, the few people who read his materials thought these ideas had no chance of success.

C. Effects

1. Those in the new middle class did not take to the streets in support of the urban poor, but they did effect change with their new political rights. For example, they convinced government leaders to provide police services and cleaner drinking water in London, build public housing in Paris, and establish unemployment and social security benefits in the new nation of Germany.

D. Irish Famine

1. Despite the technological progress that the Industrial Revolution brought, not everything it touched was an improvement.

i. In the mid-nineteenth century, steamboats hauling seed potatoes from the New World to Ireland unintentionally delivered diseased produce.

ii. Ireland was greatly dependent on the potato for food, so when the potato blight spread rapidly through its farms, about one million died and another million migrated across the Atlantic to the United States and other destinations in the Americas.

iii. Another effect of the Irish potato famine was increased support in Europe for government programs to aid the poor, not just in Ireland, but as a general policy.

III. Nationalism Leads to Revolts and Political Changes

Industrialism was not the only cause of unrest in nineteenth-century Europe. In the first half of the century, almost every nation in Europe saw violent protests supporting more political rights and nationalism.

A. "Europe in Flames"

1. The nationalist revolutions in Latin America succeeded in running off the colonial powers. These successes inspired people in Europe to try to use nationalism to throw out those governments they thought were "outside oppressors."

    i. Greece broke away from the Ottoman Empire. In the early nineteenth century, Poles, Italians, and Slavs failed in their attempt to break away from the large Austrian empire.

    ii. In 1848, so many nations experienced violence that the phrase "Europe in flames" became popular.

    iii. In the 1860s and 1870s, two new nations emerged, both forged with strong nationalist fervor: Italy and Germany.

B. More Revolts

1. In 1830 and 1848, dissatisfied French rebels overthrew their governments. In the second of these revolutions, France established another short-lived republic.

2. In Russia, in the 1820s, a military coup, promising a constitutional monarchy, failed miserably, but it inspired future revolutionaries there.

c. 1750–c. 1900 CE

IV. **European Imperialism Leads to Nationalist Movements in Africa and Asia**

A. Africa

1. Nationalism proved to be a powerful global theme in this era. Resentment over Europe's imperialist policies led to increased nationalist sentiments throughout Africa. As African elites returned from European universities, they brought back news of nationalist revolts throughout the Atlantic World.

2. The African nation with the greatest nationalist fervor in the late nineteenth century was Egypt.

   i. The Ottoman Empire, France, and England all had political and economic stakes in Egypt.

   ii. The French financed and supervised the digging of the Suez Canal in the 1860s, and jostling began almost immediately over who should receive the economic benefits from it: the Egyptians, the Ottomans, the French, or the British.

   iii. England invaded Egypt in the 1880s, claiming they were "helping" the Egyptians run their country, and stayed until the 1920s.

3. Although African nationalism had its beginnings in the nineteenth century, independence movements did not succeed until after World War II.

B. Asia

1. The best-known nationalist movement in Asia was in India against the British *raj*.

   i. The Indian National Congress was founded in the late nineteenth century with the purpose of promoting a united nationalist agenda and with the aim of gaining independence from the British.

   ii. Another nationalist movement arose in India in the early twentieth century with a different goal in mind—the Muslim League sought not all-India independence, but rather separate independence from British rule for the Muslim areas of the region.

2. In Southwest Asia and North Africa, stirrings of Arab nationalism against Ottoman and European rule began.

   i. Egypt's nationalist movement was one part of a larger Arab call for independence from the "outsiders" who were corrupting "true" Arab and Islamic culture with the decadence of the West and the decline of the Ottomans.

3. As in India, the era of Arab independence did not reach its goals until after World War II.

Test Tip | *The AP World History exam* always *asks questions about African and Asian nationalist movements.*

V. Falling Empires

A. Spain and Portugal

1. In this era, both Spain and Portugal saw their empires dwindle because of the successful independence movements in Latin America against Spanish and Portuguese rule.

2. At the end of this era, Spain's loss in the Spanish-American War effectively marked the end of that empire and the rise of the United States on the global stage.

B. The Ottoman Empire

1. While many of its European neighbors were "going global" during the Age of Imperialism, the Ottoman Empire was shrinking.

   i. Beginning with the successful nationalistic Greek rebellion for independence in the 1820s, the Ottoman Empire lost territories in the Balkan Peninsula in eastern Europe and faced growing opposition in its Arab holdings in Southwest Asia and North Africa.

ii. In addition, Russia and England fought the Crimean War over the Ottoman Empire's vital Bosporus and Dardanelles sea lanes near Constantinople. While the Ottoman Empire came out on the winning side with its British and French allies against Russia, it remained weakened, the so-called "sick man of Europe."

2. Ottoman attempts to "westernize" and compete with western Europe in the nineteenth century consisted of a movement toward a constitutional government—the Tanzimat Reforms—and the purchase of modern weapons from European manufacturers.

   i. *Tanzimat* means "reorganization," and that is what the reforms did to the Ottoman government. A written constitution with guaranteed political and social rights (including freedom of religion), a modernized banking system, railroad construction, and reorganization and modernization of the army were some of the major changes.

   ii. After 40 years under this first constitution, the Ottoman leader, the sultan, canceled it and dissolved the legislature in 1876. He did this because changes to the constitution called for limitations of the sultan's power.

3. Later, another reform movement came from within the military. The "Young Turks" were Western-educated young army officers in the early twentieth century who sought revival and extension of the Tanzimat reforms. They succeeded, but after World War I, the 700-year-old empire collapsed and was divided into many nations.

Global Migrations
c. 1750–c. 1900 CE

In the era 1750–1900, faster transportation, an increased need for labor in the global economy, and violent unrest in many parts of the world led to a period of one of the largest human migrations in world history. As the Industrial Revolution spread, more and more people took engine-powered ships and trains to new destinations. These migrations occurred within Afro-Eurasia and within the Americas, but it was the migrations to North and South America *from* Afro-Eurasia that historians focus on in this era.

I. Causes of Migration

Migrations have two overarching causes: "push" factors that make people want to leave their home, and "pull" factors that draw them to a different location.

A. Push Factors

   1. Population pressures

      i. The Industrial Revolution brought new technology, new kinds of fertilizers to farms (translation: more food), and new medicines. These factors increased—and continue to increase—populations and allow longer life spans.

      ii. India, China, and Japan were demographic centers of this push factor. People with the ability to do so often left these regions for less populated ones.

   2. Faster and cheaper transportation

      i. Reliable steamship transportation across the oceans was cheap enough for all but the poorest—provided they could get to a coastal city that had oceanic service.

3. Political unrest and religious persecution

    i. The revolutions throughout the world in the nineteenth century caused political instability and were a major push factor for migrants to leave their homelands.

    ii. An additional push factor was religious persecutions, such as the anti-Jewish pogroms in Russia.

4. Famine

    i. Along with the Irish potato famine of the mid-nineteenth century, other famines occurred in this era in East and South Asia, pushing people away from these areas.

5. Lack of employment

    i. Lack of employment, often tied to overpopulation, influenced many people to seek jobs elsewhere.

B. Pull factors

1. Urbanization

    i. Migrants gravitated to cities that had people of similar background. Italian, Jewish, German, and Chinese (to name a few) neighborhoods developed.

    ii. In addition, more government services were offered to migrants in cities than were offered to migrants in rural areas.

2. Farm land

    i. The United States, Canada, Russia, and many Latin American nations encouraged immigration with generous land policies.

        ➤ The United States offered the deed to 160 acres of farmland in the western Great Plains to settlers who survived on their land for five years.

3. Abolition of slavery

    i. The end of slavery in the Western world by the late nineteenth century did not end the need for agricultural labor.

ii. Indentured labor, a situation in which one signs on to be—for all intents and purposes—a "temporary slave," with release from obligation after a period of time—from 5 to 10 years—turned out to be a strong pulling factor for migrants from South and East Asia.

➤ Indentured servants worked on sugar plantations in the Caribbean into the 1920s. They were also significant sources of labor on islands in the Indian Ocean and in South Africa.

4. Economic opportunity

i. Many nations, especially in the New World, offered opportunities for economic advancement that were impossible in other parts of the world.

ii. Discoveries of gold in Australia, Alaska, and northwest Canada triggered "rushes" of migrants into those areas in the nineteenth and early twentieth centuries.

5. Political and religious freedom

i. Pushed out by revolutions and persecutions, migrants sought new lands hoping for greater political participation and religious tolerance.

➤ In this era, many people from southern Europe and Germany migrated to South and North America, while migrants from North Africa sought opportunities in Europe.

6. A fresh start

i. Some migrants felt pulled by the chance for a new place to start their lives again.

Test Tip

The writers of the AP World History exam are fond of questions related to migration in general and the causes and effects of migration in the industrial era in particular.

c. 1750–c. 1900 CE

Effects of Migrations

A. Changes in Demographics

1. In Africa, the European imperialist powers promoted large-scale single-crop farming for export. Huge numbers of male workers left their homelands and migrated to large farming areas, and other men sought job opportunities in Africa's larger cities.

2. Women coped by taking on responsibilities that had once been primarily "men's work," such as trade, growing crops for home use, and mining.

B. Resentment Against Migrants

1. With the huge influx of migrants came resistance from many who had established themselves previously in the "receiving" lands. Besides personal displays of prejudice, legal restrictions on migrations also began to appear, such as the 1882 Chinese Exclusion Act in the United States and the White Australian Act of 1901.

C. Sample Population Shifts

1. Through the nineteenth and into the early twentieth century, about 60 million people left Europe. Almost all went to the Americas and about 30 million of those Europeans entered the United States.

2. About 2.5 million people left China between 1850 and 1900. Most went to the United States and the western portion of South America.

3. An estimated 45 million people migrated from South Asia to Southeast Asia, along the Indian Ocean region and into the South Pacific.

4. Roughly 50 million people left western Russia and northeast Asia for Japan, Manchuria, Siberia, and Central Asia.

PERIOD 6

ACCELERATING GLOBAL CHANGE AND REALIGNMENTS

C. 1900 TO THE PRESENT

Developments in Twentieth-Century Science and the Environment

What's this? An entire period of history that covers just 1900 to now? That's right. The creators of the AP World History exam expect you to pay as much attention to the themes, trends, and events of the last century as to each of the earlier longer periods. The reason: Studying history allows us to see what the past can teach us about contemporary themes, trends, and events. You can't make those connections unless you deal with the past as well as the present. Every good history course asks you to think, "How did we get here?"

Test Tip

Be aware that 20 percent of the multiple-choice questions on the exam will cover this era. Be sure you don't rush through the twentieth-century material.

Powerful trends shaped the twentieth century: skyrocketing populations, global communications, the rise and (to a significant degree) fall of authoritarian governments, the worldwide Great Depression and its consequences, two World Wars, the rise of the United States as a global power, the fall of European hegemony, the feminist movement, the Cold War, the environmental effects of the Industrial Revolution . . . that'll do for now, but the list could go on. The thing is, for every one of these twentieth-century trends—and for that matter, for all trends throughout world history—there's always a countertrend. For example, as you'll read in Chapter 19, the increase in women's rights in many places around the world during the twentieth century has met resistance in some areas. In the early twenty-first century, there are still places where women can't vote or go to school.

This chapter addresses scientific, environmental, and population changes since 1900 and the social, political, and economic issues that accompanied them.

I. Scientific Advancements

A. Electrification of Homes and Businesses

1. Beginning in the late nineteenth century, electric power arrived in homes and businesses that were located in cities in the United States and western Europe. As the twentieth century progressed, more and more people were added to the electrical grid.

   i. Electric lights, stoves, refrigerators, and radios were among the first electric appliances that people came to take for granted in the West.

   ii. Electricity in homes and businesses changed people's sleep patterns, work patterns, and consumer choices.

   iii. By the end of the century, most of the populated world had access to electricity, but significant areas—especially in Africa—remained without lights.

B. Communication and Transportation

1. Communication

   i. Telephone

      ➤ The telephone was invented in 1876 in the United States.

      ➤ Until the 1920s in the West, it was used mainly by the rich and privileged in the "developed" countries of Europe, Australia, North and South America, and Japan.

      ➤ In the economic boom of the Roaring Twenties that occurred in most Western nations, more and more people could afford to have a telephone in their homes.

➤ Telephonic technology remained almost unchanged until the 1980s, when cell phones became available in large cities. The pattern repeated itself: At first, only wealthy people could afford cell phones, but as prices went down, availability went up. By the early twenty-first century, cell phones had become almost a necessity in the industrialized, developed world.

ii. Radio/Television

➤ Originally considered a device for one-to-one communication—a "wireless telegraph"—by the 1920s, radio networks began broadcasting entertainment and news to national audiences.

➤ Television gained popularity after World War II, so much so that by the 1960s in the United States, more homes had televisions than indoor toilets. It rapidly became more popular than radio as a means of information and entertainment.

➤ Both radio and television were used by governments to propagate their messages to citizens and foes alike.

iii. Computers and the Internet

➤ The first electronic computer was developed in the United States in the late 1940s. It took up a whole room.

➤ By the early 1980s, the first personal computers (PCs) were available to the public. PCs that are now considered antiques were originally high-priced and mysterious toys for the wealthy.

➤ Prices of PCs began to drop and their popularity began to rise with the advent of the Internet by the mid-1990s.

➤ Originally designed as a way for scientists to transmit computer data across telephone lines in the 1960s, the Internet became a global phenomenon in the early 1990s.

> ➤ By the early twenty-first century, the Internet connected billions of people and businesses, but there were still many areas with little or no Internet access, primarily in parts of Africa and Central Asia, although access was improving.

2. Transportation

   i. The Automobile

      > ➤ Automobiles were introduced in Germany in the late nineteenth century, but like radios and telephones, they did not become popular in the industrialized world until the 1920s.

      > ➤ When automobiles did become popular, they changed many aspects of Western society. One big change was the automobile's ability to make people more mobile. It became much less likely for people to live their entire lives in one place. Dating without the watchful eyes of parents became the norm. Living in the suburbs and working miles away in city centers became popular. Driving to distant vacation spots—in Europe that could mean in another country—was also possible.

      > ➤ Cars also created new industries and jobs: multinational corporations that sold petroleum products, the travel industry, and government-funded modern road construction, to name a few.

      > ➤ The automobile's popularity also led to less use of public transportation, increased rush-hour traffic, traffic fatalities, and increased air pollution.

   ii. Airplanes

      > ➤ The first application of airplanes on a wide scale was in World War I.

      > ➤ Air travel in the West was for the wealthy and famous (and military pilots) until after World War II, when an unprecedented economic boom occurred and the middle class could afford to join "the jet set."

➤ By the end of the twentieth century, passenger air travel was common in the West, but it did not surpass the use of the automobile.

➤ One casualty in many Western nations was the passenger train, which had been the most popular form of mass travel for almost 100 years.

iii. Space

➤ Liquid-fueled rockets were experimental in the 1920s and used as weapons by Germany in World War II. The Soviet Union launched the first missile to orbit the Earth in the 1950s, followed quickly by its rival, the United States.

➤ A "race to the moon" fired Cold War imaginations in the 1960s and was won by the United States.

➤ After the fall of communism in the Soviet Union in the early 1990s, the United States and Russia became partners in space exploration with a jointly run international space station.

➤ Some of the benefits of the space program include: miniaturization of electronic components, GPS systems, nonstick coating on cooking utensils, medical imaging (for example, PET scans), among others.

C. Scientific Understanding Alters Society's Views of the World

1. After the Scientific Revolution in the seventeenth century, people's "faith" in science in the West reached a level where even scientific theories affected society itself.

i. After Darwin published his theory of evolution in *On the Origin of Species* in 1859, major debates ensued in Western society.

ii. In the early twentieth century, the German mathematician Albert Einstein contributed to the theory of relativity.

➤ In basic terms, his theory overturned Newton's ideas about a constant universe and postulated instead that space and time can vary, depending on the point of view of the observer.

➤ In this new view of the universe and humanity's place in it, there are no absolutes.

➤ This view of the universe had tremendous impact on Western society after World War I.

➤ The "great civilized powers" of Europe had set out to destroy each other in World War I with weapons produced by the Industrial Revolution, and about 20 million people were killed. Newton's view of an ordered, rational universe didn't make sense any more.

➤ Philosophers, artists, composers, and theologians took the scientific concept of relativity and applied it to society. Right and wrong were no longer absolutes but instead were concepts for each individual to determine.

D. Medical Technologies Extended Life Expectancy

1. Throughout world history, infant mortality was the greatest factor in limiting life expectancy. Children who survived past their fifth birthday could generally expect to live into their sixties.

2. The results of systematic scientific research from universities, hospitals, and medical-related corporations were medicines, healthier lifestyles, and surgical techniques that greatly increased life expectancy in the twentieth century.

   i. The polio vaccine, antibiotics, improved surgical procedures such as sterilizing equipment, and advances in cancer treatments all contributed.

   ii. Deadly infectious diseases such as smallpox and whooping cough were virtually eliminated through global campaigns of inoculation, yet other diseases developed and spread.

3. These medical advances were largely limited, however, to industrialized nations. In 2011, for example, 26 nations with the lowest life expectancy were in Africa.

E. Developments in Energy Sources

1. Fossil fuels

    i.   Coal was used as an energy source around the world for many centuries, but the Industrial Revolution's powerful machines demanded unprecedented amounts of fuel.

    ii. Diesel and gasoline, refined from petroleum ("rock oil") in the second half of the nineteenth century, were found to be even more efficient fuels, and industrial production increased even more.

    iii. Like coal, processing petroleum products can damage the environment. Throughout the twentieth century, governments and fuel-related businesses struggled to find a balance between society's demands for these fuels and the health of the environment.

    iv. By the end of this era, despite some implementation of other forms of energy such as solar and wind power, fossil fuels remained the cheapest and most widely used source of energy.

2. Nuclear energy

    i.   The struggle over the use of atomic energy power plants was particularly intense. In the 1950s, in the Western nations and in the Soviet Union, atomic energy was promoted as the clean, efficient energy source of the future, but over time it lost favor.

    ii. In 1979, a nuclear plant in the United States narrowly avoided a nuclear disaster.

    iii. In 1986 in the USSR, the Chernobyl nuclear facility exploded, creating unprecedented destruction from a nonmilitary atomic source.

    iv. In 2011, an earthquake and tsunami struck nuclear power plants in Japan, and an explosion occurred. This event has been dubbed the worst nuclear meltdown

C. 1900 TO THE PRESENT

since Chernobyl but the full extent of damage, human health effects and environmental impacts will not be known for several years.

v. Nations and individuals sought alternative forms of energy such as solar and wind power, but by the early twenty-first century, they were far behind fossil fuels in terms of electrical output.

II. Environment

It is important that you understand that the "environment" in AP World History does not refer to just trees, birds, and rivers. People and their interactions with the environment are integral parts. More people make more demands for more food crops and require more housing for shelter.

A. Global Population Soared During the Twentieth Century

1. Because of better medicine, plentiful food, and healthier habits, people lived longer in the twentieth century than ever before.

    i. Longer life tends to mean more children.

    ii. Population growth zoomed in the twentieth century, with few signs of abatement by the early twenty-first century. (See the chart that follows.)

    iii. The highest numbers of people were concentrated in South and East Asia, which has been the norm for thousands of years.

2. Concerns over high population rates led some nations—China and India, in particular—to initiate government policies to limit the number of births.

    i. China enacted a "one-child policy" aimed at urban couples. By the year 2000, China's population was over 1 billion.

ii. India's government adopted a national population policy, which incorporated many attempts to curb birth rates, but its population continued to climb.

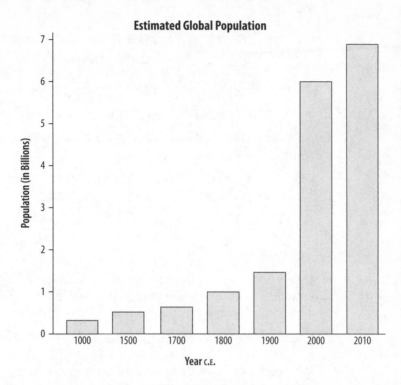

Estimated Global Population

The AP World History exam has been known to include questions about global population numbers, especially after the discovery of the Americas by Europeans and after the Industrial Revolution.

B. Innovations in Farming Led to a So-Called Green Revolution

1. In the mid-twentieth century, the development of powerful fertilizers and pesticides combined with new high-yield, disease-resistant crops led to predictions of a famine-free world.

   i. The Green Revolution held out hope that food could be grown almost anywhere.

   ii. Although food production skyrocketed during the Green Revolution, so did the global population.

  2. India was an early participant in the Green Revolution in the 1960s.

   i. New hybrid rice crops grown in combination with strong pesticides produced very high yields, so much so that India seemed to end its long cycle of periodic famine and became a leader in rice exports.

   ii. Corn and wheat were other popular hybrid crops.

  3. Attempts to spread the Green Revolution yielded mixed results.

   i. In the Philippines, rice yields soared, but in much of Africa, agricultural production stagnated.

   ii. Shifting weather patterns contributed to Africa's lower crop yield, as have the destructive nature of many civil wars since the end of World War II.

  4. Despite the setbacks, the amount of food grown globally increased tremendously because of the Green Revolution—and so has global population.

  5. Criticisms of the Green Revolution included environmental concerns about overuse of pesticides and fertilizers, the tendency of farmers to plant monocrops instead of a variety of grains as they once had, and unprecedented population growth. More food means more people can eat and thus live and reproduce. But from a long-term global perspective, experts wonder whether the Green Revolution can continue to feed ever-increasing numbers of people.

C. Pollution

  1. With the benefits of enormous industrial growth also came pollution of the environment on levels not seen before. Pollution such as wastewater or smoke from fires has always been part of human society, but mass production of goods often meant mass production of waste products getting into surrounding rivers, ground, and air.

    i.   In 1970, a grassroots pro-environment movement led to more government regulation of industrial pollution in the capitalist West.

    ii. After the fall of communism in eastern Europe in the late twentieth century, there were revelations of massive amounts of industrial pollution, unlike anything seen in the West.

III. **War, Disease, and Famine**

War and disease have always been significant causes of human fatalities. It would seem logical that a century that saw an unparalleled surge in population would also have high numbers of deaths. But the era 1900 to the present seemed to outdo nature itself in the area of human casualties.

A. War

  1. World War I introduced mass-production techniques to the battlefield.

    i.   Machine guns firing as many as 600 bullets per second could kill thousands of people in an afternoon. Estimates are as many as 8 million soldiers and 12 million civilians died in World War I.

    ii. In the Russian civil war of 1918–1920, perhaps 20 million more people died.

  2. Twenty years later, World War II showed that improved military technology, such as massive bombing campaigns against large cities, could be even more destructive.

    i.   In World War II, over 20 million people died in Russia alone, and roughly 60 million died worldwide.

    ii. The elimination of the Japanese cities of Hiroshima and Nagasaki with atomic bombs began an era where instant annihilation on a massive scale was possible.

iii. As in all wars, most of the civilian deaths were not a result of battlefield conflict but rather of disease and famine.

B. Disease

1. The first truly global disease epidemic was partly a result of World War I. The 1918 influenza pandemic killed roughly 20 million people worldwide. It is thought that returning soldiers carried the disease to their home countries around the globe, with devastating effects. Through the course of the twentieth century, new strains of flu occurred from time to time, but they did not have the impact of the 1918 version.

2. HIV/AIDS was the second major pandemic of the twentieth century—as many as 25 million people died from the disease by the early twenty-first century.

    i. First identified in the late twentieth century, HIV spread through sexual contact and needle sharing, the latter usually by people using illicit drugs. It then entered undetected into hospital blood supplies and was transmitted via transfusions.

    ii. Once it entered the societies of Central Africa, it was—and continues to be—highly destructive.

    iii. AIDS is a leading cause of death in Africa. In 2007, 2.8 million people died from AIDS—2 million of those were in Africa. Government programs promoting both abstinence and safe sex had limited success in that continent.

C. Famine

1. One result of modern war on civilian populations is a disruption of the food supply.

   i.   Famine struck Europe after World War I.

   ii. Most of the 20 million deaths in the Russian civil war are attributed to famine.

2. Government policies of keeping food away from those deemed an enemy of the state killed many millions in the twentieth century.

   i.   In the 1930s, Stalin enacted an "artificial famine" against rural communities that resisted his rule in the USSR, and approximately 13 million died.

   ii. In the mid-twentieth century, Mao's insistence on industrial over agricultural production caused perhaps 20 million deaths in China.

3. Natural disasters such as droughts and floods in China, India, and East Africa killed still more millions in the era 1900 to the present. High population densities in East and South Asia increased death tolls due to these causes, despite international assistance campaigns.

World Conflicts and Their Effects

c. 1900 to the Present

The twentieth century began with Europeans occupying empires around the globe and confident that things would stay that way. In 1900, the United States and Japan were rising powers, while Russia and China were crumbling from within. Two world wars and one global cold war later, European hegemony had declined dramatically, and China's power was rapidly rising. What a difference a century can make! Between those historical bookends, European colonies around the world gained independence and Russia became the first of many communist nations. After World War II, the Union of Soviet Socialist Republics (USSR) and the United States led their allies through decades of global tensions. At the beginning of the twenty-first century, Cold War worries had faded, but new challenges to political, social, and economic stability emerged.

I. Global Conflicts Shake World Stability

World historians often look at the two World Wars as one event with a pause in the middle. Other major wars in history had similar patterns. For example, the Crusades and the Hundred Years' War took long "timeouts" before restarting hostilities.

Test Tip

> *The AP European History and AP U.S. History exams go into greater depth regarding the World Wars, while the AP World History exam focuses more on their global causes and consequences.*

A. World War I (1914–1918)

When World War I ended in 1918, the survivors prayed that it would indeed be the "war to end all wars." No war involving Europe had ever caused so much widespread destruction of lives, property, and empires. The creation of a global League of Nations at the war's end, designed to keep the peace, gave many people hope that governments and individuals had learned their lesson and would find ways to avoid future wars. Their hopes were short-lived.

1. Causes of World War I

   i. Imperialism

      ➤ By the end of the nineteenth century, the colonial powers of Europe had competed for decades over land in Africa and Asia. By the beginning of the twentieth century, wrangling continued over ever-diminishing amounts of unclaimed territories, leading to increased competitions and suspicions among European nations.

   ii. Nationalism

      ➤ Tensions rose inside the Austro-Hungarian Empire, the Ottoman Empire, and the Russian Empire from ethnic groups that wanted to break off and form their own nations. In addition, leaders of the newly unified nations, such as Germany and Italy, naturally had great pride in their countries and expressed it through imperialist expansion and weapons buildup.

   iii. Arms race

      ➤ The Industrial Revolution spurred the mass production of weapons that could kill at faster rates, and from longer distances, than ever before. The French developed a machine gun that could shoot 300 bullets a minute, and the Germans built a cannon that could fire projectiles over 50 miles. National pride among the "Great Powers" of Europe started an unofficial competition among governments to see who could produce the best weapons.

iv. Alliance system

➤ Rather than risk going it alone in armed conflict, the Great Powers formed two competing military alliances in the early twentieth century: Russia, England, and France formed the *Triple Entente* and Germany, Italy, and Austria-Hungary formed the *Triple Alliance*. Geographically, the Entente was positioned on Germany's eastern and western borders, leading that nation's leaders to develop "first strike" plans in both directions.

v. All these factors (imperialism, nationalism, the arms race, and the alliance system) led to heightened tensions in Europe by 1914.

➤ The event that sparked World War I was the assassination of the future emperor of Austria-Hungary in Bosnia, a province that was teeming with nationalist independence fervor. A chain of reactions to the assassination led to a realignment of the prewar alliances into two slightly different groups: the Allies, initially England, France, Russia, and Italy, and the Central Powers of Germany, Austria-Hungary, and the Ottoman Empire.

vi. The Central Powers had short-term advantages at the start of World War I:

➤ They were connected geographically, whereas the Allies were separated.

➤ Germany had the best trained and best equipped army in the world going into the war.

➤ The German industrial system was better suited for conversion to wartime production than were those of the Allies.

vii. The Allies had long-term advantages at the start of World War I:

> ➤ The Allies had more men of military age than did the Central Powers.

> ➤ The Allies had more factories, but converting them to war production took time.

> ➤ The Allies had a stronger navy and therefore were able to enforce a blockade of the ports of the Central Powers.

2. Features of World War I

   i. No one expected a long war. Germany attacked France and Russia simultaneously, expecting a quick victory that would establish Germany as the unquestioned power in Europe.

   > ➤ When that did not occur, the two sides hunkered down into defensive positions in France (the Western Front) and Russia (the Eastern Front) by the end of 1914.

   > ➤ By 1915, fighting spread to the Ottoman Empire and the European colonies in Africa.

   ii. The new weapons of World War I—including the machine gun, poison gas, the airplane, and the submarine—led to changes in tactics and philosophies about the rules of war.

   > ➤ The machine gun's rapid killing power forced combatants on all sides into defensive trenches, but despite the enormous losses, military leaders repeatedly sent long lines of men charging across "No Man's Land," the open fields that lay between the opponents.

   > ➤ The result was four years of shocking numbers of deaths and injuries. In the Battle of the Somme in France, 20,000 British soldiers died the first day, and 60,000 died before the first soldier reached the German trenches. After four months of continuous battle, about 1.5 million men from both sides were killed, wounded, missing, or captured.

➤ An unintended consequence of this kind of slaughter was a lowering of the value of humanity in war. Civilians came to be considered legitimate targets in "total war"—where the full economic production and political power of nations were engaged in military victory. Submarines torpedoed enemy civilian ships—like the British steamship *Lusitania*—and cannons indiscriminately fired huge artillery shells into cities far away.

iii. One effect of European global colonization was the use of soldiers recruited from Africa and Asia to fight in the war.

➤ India committed one million troops to aid the British forces.

➤ Military campaigns ensued in the colonies, especially in Africa, where German soldiers and their African recruits battled British and French soldiers and their African recruits.

➤ Australian soldiers joined their British counterparts at the failed Allied assault on Gallipoli, in the Ottoman Empire.

➤ The British also convinced Arabs to unite with them against the Ottomans in Southwest Asia, promising Arab independence from the Ottomans as a reward.

iv. In 1917, the United States entered World War I on the Allies' side "to make the world safe for democracy," an idealistic pledge made by U.S. President Woodrow Wilson.

➤ By late 1918, the addition of U.S. soldiers pushed the Central Powers to the breaking point, and an armistice was signed. An *armistice* is an agreement that all sides will lay down their arms and leave the battlefield without declaring a winner—or loser.

➤ Wilson hoped for "peace without victory," believing that punishing Germany after the war would lead to resentment and another war.

After the fighting stopped, however, England and France declared themselves the winners and Germany the loser.

v. President Wilson proposed the Fourteen Points plan, designed to stop future wars through a checklist of international agreements. The key component was an international organization—the League of Nations—that was set up to settle differences between member nations before they erupted into armed conflict. The U.S. Congress refused to join the very League that Wilson created. Thus, the League was crippled from the outset.

3. Consequences of World War I

i. Approximately 20 million soldiers and civilians died in the war, which was fought in Europe, Southwest Asia, and Africa. The political, social, and economic impact of the loss of so many people shaped many Europeans' attitudes about war for the next two decades. In the 1930s, for example, a large number of citizens and politicians in England and France favored appeasement, giving in to an aggressor nation rather than challenging it and risking war.

ii. The Treaty of Versailles approved the League of Nations but, yielding to pressures from angry citizens back home, the leaders of England and France also dictated terms to the Central Powers and focused on punishing Germany (so much for "peace without victory"). Germany was required to take full blame for starting the war, drastically reduce its military forces, and pay billions in war reparations to England and France.

➤ Many German people developed a strong sense of resentment toward the Allied nations, especially after their economy imploded in the 1920s due to harsh reparation demands from the English and French.

➤ The German currency, the mark, plummeted from a rate of four to the dollar in 1914 to over a *trillion* to the dollar by late 1923.

➤ The Allies required Germany to ditch its constitutional monarchy and set up a republic—known as the Weimar Republic.

➤ The government was too frail and fragmented to deal effectively with the unprecedented economic crisis. These events caused many Germans to seek radical alternatives to the Weimar Republic and to seek revenge against England and France.

iii. Several international treaties between the World Wars sought to limit the expansion of military might and thus reduce the chance of war.

➤ The Five Power Treaty, the London Conference of 1930, the Geneva Conventions, and the Kellogg-Briand Pact were the most famous.

➤ The first two treaties limited the number of battleships each nation could have. Japan rejected the limits because it was allotted fewer ships than the United States and England.

➤ The Geneva Conventions set rules for war, particularly the treatment of prisoners of war.

iv. Many of the African and Middle Eastern colonies controlled by Germany and the Ottoman Empire were reassigned by the League of Nations to France and England, who established a mandate system of rule over them.

➤ Under this system, France and England were to guide the Middle Eastern colonies of Syria and Lebanon (France), Palestine and Jordan (England), and Iraq (England) until the League decided the colonies were ready for independence.

➤ The reality of the situation was that these areas were simply added to the British and French colonial collection.

➤ African mandates formally under German control were southwest Africa and Tanganyika.

➤ These moves prompted more nationalist feelings in the people living in the colonies in the Middle East and Africa, and also in Southeast Asia.

v. The Russian, Austrian, Ottoman, and German empires fell during or just after World War I.

➤ Austria's once-huge empire was divided into several nations, including Yugoslavia, Hungary, and a smaller Austria.

➤ The democratic nation of Turkey was established by nationalists led by Mustafa Kemal, who went by the title "Ataturk."

vi. Two Allied nations, the United States and Japan, emerged from the war with their industrial capacity and colonial possessions intact, unlike most of Europe, and were poised to rise to the top of the world's economic ladder.

vii. Conducting the war amidst rising internal problems proved too much for the Russian czar's government.

➤ In 1917, the czar resigned and was replaced by a provisional democracy. But it quickly fell to a communist uprising.

➤ Bolshevik leader Vladimir Lenin negotiated an early withdrawal from the war with the German government and thus fighting on the eastern front ended.

➤ As payback for quitting the war early (and because they feared the new communist government), the other Allied powers pretended Russia had never been on their side and refused to give them a seat at Versailles.

viii. Arming their colonial subjects to support the war effort may not have been in Europe's best interest because at the end of the war, nationalist leaders in African and Asian colonies had military training and equipment.

➤ Adding to their inclinations toward independence, many elites had learned about European ideals, such as self-rule, while attending European schools before the war.

> ➤ Another encouragement for leaders of colonial independence movements was found in a key feature of the Fourteen Points plan—a call for "self-determination" for nationalist groups. This Wilsonian concept was specifically intended for groups in Europe, but none of the colonial subjects in Africa or Asia worried about that detail.

ix. World War I ended with many issues unresolved: What would be the future of European imperialism around the world? Could Western nations slow the spread of military technology to the colonies? How would Europe handle colonial nationalist movements? In addition, new issues that didn't exist before the war included what to do about a newly communist Russian nation and how to recover from the economic, political, and social damages wrought by World War I.

B. World War II (1939–1945)

1. Causes of World War II

    i. Primarily a continuation of unresolved issues from World War I, World War II outdid its predecessor in duration, global scope, use of military technology, and death.

    > ➤ The Treaty of Versailles required Germany to accept full guilt for the war, reduce its military forces, hand over its colonies, and pay billions in war reparations to England and France. Germany, however, was rocked by overwhelming economic collapse. These humiliations left many Germans seeking vengeance.

    > ➤ One man in particular, Adolf Hitler, tapped into these emotions and exploited them as a means of gaining power.

    ii. Starting in late 1929, the Great Depression shook the foundations of the global economy. However, western

European nations had suffered all through the decade after the war.

➤ The United States was the chief financer of England, France, and Germany's debts in the 1920s, and when those nations struggled to repay their loans, U.S. banks began to falter, setting off chain reactions that damaged global financial markets.

➤ Another cause of the Great Depression was overproduction of goods in the United States—especially farm products. More produce meant lower prices to farmers; lower prices meant farmers defaulted on bank loans, banks closed, and money supplies dried up.

iii. The result in the industrialized nations was that, in the 1930s, they all reorganized their governments to be more active in financial matters, including government programs of social security, unemployment compensation, bank regulation, and many others.

➤ Italy, Germany, and Japan were the most prominent nations that radically changed their governmental and financial systems. These systems were changed to *fascism* to address the economic crises in these three countries.

➤ Russia—known as the Soviet Union after 1922—was isolated from the global economy. Europe and the United States wanted nothing to do with the new communist government.

iv. Italy introduced *fascism* in the 1920s as a political and social means to address its post–World War I economic woes.

➤ Under fascism, the government attempted to control the economy—which was also the case in communism—but it allowed private ownership of businesses and other property—as was the case in capitalism. One catch—all decisions ultimately came from a single dictator with enormous power, and dissent was severely punished. Anyone considered "outside" the accepted fascist model faced unemployment, jail, or death.

➤ Before the international meltdown of the Great Depression, Italy's fascist system—led by Benito Mussolini—appeared to be on an upswing in the 1920s.

➤ Fascism appealed to many people around the world—Germany, Spain, and then Japan followed Italy's political model.

v. In Germany, nazism was Adolf Hitler's version of fascism. The National Socialist (abbreviated "Nazi") German Workers' Party was a fringe group in the early 1920s, at a time when the Weimar Republic was floundering. It claimed opposition to both democracy on one hand and communism on the other, and promoted past and future German glories.

vi. Fascism requires conquest to obtain cheap labor and raw materials—and to unite its people against enemies, real or invented.

➤ Except for Spain, the fascist nations of the twentieth century attacked their neighbors.

➤ Italy invaded North Africa and Ethiopia in the 1930s.

➤ Germany invaded Czechoslovakia and Austria about the same time.

vii. Japan began attacking its neighbors even before it officially turned to fascism. Some historians argue that World War II really started in 1931—eight years before the official date—when Japan invaded Manchuria, enslaved or killed its people, and occupied their coal mines and factories. Not satisfied with that conquest alone, Japan invaded China in 1937.

viii. The well-intentioned but weak League of Nations did little to stop aggression by Italy, Germany, and Japan in the 1930s. European leaders hoped that fascists would be satisfied after limited conquests and seek no more territories.

> ➤ This policy of appeasement only seemed to encourage the attackers, who showed no respect for the League of Nations' pleas for peace.

> ➤ The appeasement policy of the 1930s had long-term effects: After World War II, one of the biggest lessons the United States and the USSR took from the prewar era was to reject appeasement in favor of "peace through strength" during the confrontational Cold War.

2. Features of World War II

   i. Like World War I, there were two sets of alliances in World War II: the Allies and the Axis Powers.

   > ➤ Germany, Italy, and Japan formed the Axis starting in the late 1930s.

   > ➤ England, France, Poland, and most of western Europe formed the Allies by 1940. The Allies grew in number as they were attacked by Axis nations.

   > ➤ A year later, the USSR and the United States joined the Allies.

   ii. Unlike World War I, which featured trench warfare and little movement of forces, World War II began with fast-moving fronts. This change occurred because technology improved the machines that were introduced in World War I.

   > ➤ Tanks and airplanes moved much faster by the 1930s, and defensive trenches were impractical.

   > ➤ Germany introduced the *blitzkrieg* ("lightning war"), which involved bombing from airplanes and swift advances by tanks and support vehicles. Only then did foot soldiers enter the battle—if there were still people left to fight back. This method of fighting stunned early victims of Nazi aggression.

iii. In the European theater, the war started in 1939 when Germany invaded Poland. England had appeased the German fascist dictator Hitler in his conquest of central Europe, but it finally drew a line at Poland.

➤ After war was declared, Germany swiftly conquered most of western Europe, including France, by 1940.

➤ Russia and Germany had announced a peace treaty in 1939, so England faced Nazi aggression alone.

➤ Two significant events in 1941 turned the tide against Nazi Germany: Hitler's surprise invasion of Russia went poorly, and the United States entered the war against the Axis Powers after Japan attacked Pearl Harbor.

➤ Unlike its position in World War I, Russia stayed with the Allies to the end of the war, despite suffering more than 25 million deaths.

iv. The first Allied offensive against the Axis Powers was in North Africa. From there, the Allies invaded Italy but were still fighting there when the war in Europe ended.

➤ The turning point of the war in Europe was the Allied invasion of Normandy (in France) in 1944. Steadily pushed back to their homeland on both the eastern and western fronts, the Germans surrendered in May 1945.

v. World War II's battlefields were on a greater global scale than were those of World War I.

➤ Campaigns throughout the Pacific were added to those in Europe and Africa.

➤ Japan's attack on China from 1937 to 1945 was particularly brutal, causing approximately 20 million deaths.

➤ In addition, in 1941, Japan attacked much of Southeast Asia and islands throughout the Pacific, including Hawaii's Pearl Harbor in 1941. The

United States entered the Pacific war and, with Britain as its main ally, slowly pushed the Japanese empire's perimeter back toward its homeland.

➤ In August 1945, the United States dropped two atomic bombs, first on Hiroshima and then on Nagasaki, and the war abruptly stopped.

3. Consequences of World War II

i. The United Nations (UN) replaced the League of Nations after World War II.

➤ Two key differences: the UN's headquarters was in the United States, not Europe—a sign of the United States' postwar influence—and, unlike the League, the United Nations Security Council had military authority that could be used to stop aggression by nations.

➤ UN forces were employed in combat in the Korean War (1950–1953) and the Persian Gulf War (1990–1991).

ii. The use of atomic power was a major controversy after World War II.

➤ Military and government supporters of its use on Japan claimed its overwhelming destruction saved lives that would have been lost in a conventional attack on Japan's homeland.

➤ Critics questioned the morality of its use at all and raised concerns about the specter of a world armed with nuclear weapons.

iii. Western Europe's reign as the world's strongest economic and political force ended with World War II.

➤ Two devastating wars crippled Europe, while the United States emerged as the only major power whose economy and society was relatively unscathed.

➤ Aided by the United Nations, Europe's colonies in Africa and Asia gained independence, one by one, starting soon after the war. These colonies included the Dutch East Indies, Indochina, India, and Ghana.

iv. The Holocaust was the worst fascist treatment of "outsiders." Hitler's "final solution" targeted Jews and other groups that did not fit into his perverted vision for Germany. Six million of the 10 million people killed in the Holocaust were Jews from central and eastern Europe.

> ➤ After the war, the United States and Britain steered UN support for the establishment of a democratic Jewish homeland (Israel) in Palestine.

v. The Cold War started almost immediately after World War II. Global tensions arose between the victorious Allies, with the USSR leading one side and the United States leading the other.

C. The Cold War (c. 1946–c.1989)

1. The conflict that best meets the description of "World War III" was the Cold War.

   i. The capitalist United States and its allies in the West competed with the communist USSR and its allies for global superiority.

   ii. What made it a "cold" war was that the main antagonists did not fight each other directly on a battlefield. However, everything else involved in a "hot" war was in play: threats of destruction, gathering of military allies, arms buildup, spy networks, and propaganda campaigns. Even the exploration of outer space and Olympic competitions were part of the Cold War.

   iii. The addition of nuclear weapons in this era made the outcome of any such war extremely hazardous to the entire world.

2. Causes of the Cold War

   i.   The Yalta Conference.

   ➤ Near the end of World War II, the "Big Three" Allies (the United States, Britain, and the USSR) met on the Crimean peninsula to redraw the maps of Europe and Asia for the postwar world.

   ➤ Germany and its capital, Berlin, were divided into Western and Soviet regions.

   ➤ The USSR took control of most of eastern Europe (now a separate entity from western Europe), after promising the United States and Britain it would allow self-determination.

   ➤ When that pledge failed to materialize and Soviet forces began to occupy eastern Europe, the West became highly suspicious of Soviet intentions.

   ➤ For its part, leaders in the USSR feared a U.S.-led invasion through Germany or Japan.

   ii. The Yalta Conference also divided Korea into communist north and capitalist south nations. Japan was put into the U.S. sphere of influence. The United States replaced Japan's government with a democratic constitutional monarchy and placed military bases there.

   iii. The USSR gained nuclear weapons a few years after the end of World War II. This event stirred great concern among the Western allies, but the Soviet Union claimed the weapons were for self-defense purposes.

3. Features of the Cold War

   i.   Led by the United States, NATO and its allies enacted a diplomatic and military policy of containment to keep the Soviets from spreading communism beyond Eastern Europe. World events challenged this policy around the globe for 45 years.

   ii. The Berlin Airlift

   ➤ In 1946, the USSR attempted to cut off Western access to Berlin, which was in Soviet-controlled

East Germany. For a year, the United States and Britain flew supplies into the Western sector of Berlin. The Soviets realized the futility of their blockade and lifted it.

➤ This event increased Cold War tensions between the two sides. In 1961, communist East Germany built a wall dividing the pro-West sector of Berlin from its communist half.

➤ The Berlin Wall lasted until 1989, when anticommunist East Berliners rose up and began tearing it down on live television.

iii. The Marshall Plan

➤ As part of the U.S. containment doctrine to limit the expansion of communism, and to help its Western European allies recover from the war, the United States sent billions of dollars in economic and construction aid to West Germany, England, France, and other western European nations. Japan also received massive amounts of reconstruction assistance.

➤ The Marshall Plan was lauded as a "brilliant success" that rebuilt factories and roads.

➤ By the early 1950s, Western Europe and Japan had booming economies.

➤ The USSR attempted a similar aid package for Eastern Europe called Comecon, but its efforts were less successful.

iv. NATO versus the Warsaw Pact

➤ In 1949, the United States formed an alliance with western European nations called the North Atlantic Treaty Organization (NATO). It was designed to contain Soviet aggression in Europe. Canada and Turkey were also included.

➤ The USSR responded with a military alliance of its own, the Warsaw Pact, which most eastern European nations were compelled to join.

C. 1900 TO THE PRESENT

➤ For decades, most experts assumed World War III would be fought in central Europe—probably over East or West Germany—between these two sides. Almost no forecasters in the 1960s and 1970s expected the USSR to disintegrate by the early 1990s.

v. Led by Mao Zedong, communists took control of China in 1949. The twentieth century Chinese Revolutions and China's Cold War relationship with the USSR and the West are discussed in more depth later in this chapter.

vi. The Korean War

➤ In 1950, communist North Korea invaded pro-West South Korea and, for the first time, the United Nations sent soldiers from member nations to push out the aggressor.

➤ The United States led the UN forces in this war, which included a surprise massive surge from communist Chinese soldiers into Korea.

➤ After three years of constant fighting, the adversaries negotiated new boundaries of the two Koreas near their previous borders. The United States and its military allies announced a global plan of containment designed to keep communism from spreading beyond its 1950 borders.

vii. The Vietnam War

➤ Just after World War II, a war for independence in French colonial Indochina became a Cold War battle for that region, which was divided in the early 1950s into four nations, including pro-communist North Vietnam (led by Ho Chi Min), pro-West South Vietnam, Laos, and Cambodia.

➤ Much like in Korea, North Vietnam soon invaded South Vietnam to unify the country under communist rule. Vietnam became the focus of U.S. containment policy, and the U.S. government committed its military to fighting a limited war until running out of resolve.

➤ In 1975, the communists of North Vietnam defeated and absorbed South Vietnam, creating a unified socialist nation. Hundreds of thousands of South Vietnamese migrated to France, Australia, and the United States over the next two decades to escape the communist system.

viii. In Latin America, Cold War tensions were at their peak during the Cuban Missile Crisis in 1962.

➤ Cuba became a communist nation in 1959. In the early 1960s, the USSR secretly placed missiles with nuclear capability there. The United States discovered the missiles and brought the issue to the United Nations. On the brink of a nuclear war, cooler heads prevailed and the crisis eased.

➤ A direct line of communication was created to link the White House in the United States and Soviet offices in Moscow, and the USSR removed the controversial missiles.

➤ In the late 1970s and early 1980s, guerilla wars in Latin America between pro- and anticommunist forces involved U.S. and Soviet military "advisors."

ix. Other so-called brush wars between pro-West and pro-Soviet bloc interests erupted in Africa and Central Asia during the Cold War.

4. Consequences of the Cold War

i. Cost

➤ The Cold War involved expenditures of many billions of dollars on both sides, especially by the main antagonists: the United States and the USSR.

➤ Proponents argue that the money spent was much less than what would have been appropriated if there had been a hot war between the rivals, not to mention the cost in human lives.

     ii. Nuclear legacy

➤ The enormous destructive nature of nuclear bombs may well have been the deciding factor in the Cold War remaining cold. The major rivals may have avoided using nuclear weapons, but after the Cold War, many nations developed or tried to build their own nuclear arsenal.

➤ Few of them responded to calls from the United States, the former USSR, or the United Nations to curtail their nuclear programs.

➤ India, Pakistan, Israel, and Iran are some examples of countries that have developed their own nuclear programs.

Test Tip

The features and consequences of the Cold War have appeared on every AP World History exam.

D. The Post–Cold War World, c. 1989 to the Present

  1. Decline of communism

    i. Under the leadership of Soviet President Mikhail Gorbachev and pushed along by a military buildup by U.S. President Ronald Reagan, the USSR softened its strict communist philosophies and military aggression by the mid-1980s. These events gave rise to anti-Soviet and prodemocracy movements in Eastern Europe.

    ii. The success of these movements was symbolized by the uncontested tearing down of the Berlin Wall in 1989.

   iii. Faced with a failing economy, loss of international prestige, nationalist revolts from within the Soviet Union, and an attempt by members of his own government to overthrow him in a coup attempt, Gorbachev announced the breakup of the USSR in 1991, and a Russian Federation was established.

iv. The thirteen non-Russian members of the USSR split off to form their own governments.

2. The decline of communism and its authoritarian methods affected Latin America in that most military dictatorships were replaced by democratic governments starting in the 1980s. Argentina and Chile are two examples.

3. Not all political movements were in the direction of democratic rule after the Cold War.

   i. In the Middle East, dictatorships and kingdoms remained in some nations—for example, in Saudi Arabia and Iran.

   ii. In China, a prodemocracy movement led by students in 1989 was brutally crushed by the government in Beijing's Tiananmen Square, even as the communist regime there was permitting limited capitalism.

Test Tip

The AP World History exam rarely asks questions about political events after the end of the Cold War.

II. Decolonization

Europe was weakened after two world wars. A major sign of Europe's decline as a world power was successful colonial independence movements after World War II. Some colonies gained independence peacefully, but others gained independence with violent revolutions. By the mid-1970s, almost all former European colonies returned to local control. Decolonization is one of the major themes of the twentieth century.

A. Asia

1. The first major colony to gain independence after World War II was also the largest, India.

   i. Mohandas Gandhi led nonviolent resistance to the British *raj* for decades, supported by the Indian National

Congress and the Muslim League. Their efforts were successful in 1947, but Gandhi's dream of a united, independent India was not fulfilled.

    ii. Muslim-majority areas, such as Pakistan and Bangladesh, formed separate nations in what was known as *the partition of India.*

2. The Dutch East Indies and Indochina represent two colonies that rebelled violently for independence.

    ➤ The Netherlands granted independence to the new nation of Indonesia in 1965.

    ➤ France granted independence after Indochina split into four nations: Laos, Cambodia, and North and South Vietnam.

3. Hong Kong did not gain independence, but the British peacefully transferred sovereignty of Hong Kong—which it had held since the Opium Wars—to communist China in 1997 on the promise that the island would remain a capitalist haven.

B. Africa

1. North African nations tended to gain independence from European control earlier than sub-Saharan nations.

    i. In the 1950s, the United Nations supported the peaceful independence of Libya and Tunisia.

    ii. The most significant rebellion in North Africa occurred in Algeria, where French soldiers battled nationalist rebels until France granted independence in 1962.

2. Ghana was the first sub-Saharan colony to gain independence, peacefully, in 1957.

3. Angolan rebels, aided by the USSR, China, and Cuba, fought against Portuguese rule until Angola became independent in 1975.

4. Most other African colonies gained freedom through peaceful means and with support from the United Nations.

C. Latin America

1. In Latin America, Europe's few colonies gained independence in the postwar era as well. The Bahamas and the Guiana colonies are two examples.

D. Outcomes of Decolonization

1. Some former colonies had economic success and political stability after decolonization—India, Singapore, and Indonesia are three examples.

    i. However, many colonies struggled, facing civil wars, crumbling infrastructures, and continued economic hardships. Malawi and Zaire are but two examples in Africa alone.

    ii. One continuity over the centuries has been Africa's lack of industrial production. It remained an exporter primarily of natural resources such as oil, gold, and other minerals.

2. South Africa wasn't a colony per se. It became an independent country in 1910, but it retained strong political and economic ties to Britain.

    i. South Africa had a long-standing policy of white minority rule called *apartheid*. Under apartheid, whites of Dutch, German, and British descent had full political rights, but the majority black and mixed-race population had none for most of the twentieth century.

    ii. The government yielded to increasing international pressure and transitioned to constitutional rights for all citizens, regardless of color, in the 1990s.

III. **The Rise and Decline of Authoritarian Governments, c. 1900 to the Present**

In the early twenty-first century, plenty of authoritarian governments existed (and continue to exist) around the world, but the

C. **1900** TO THE PRESENT

high point of communist and fascist dictatorships was during the twentieth century. Proposed by Marx in England in 1848, communism did not take hold as a government until the early twentieth century. Russia was first to adopt communism, and many other nations—most significantly China—adopted it after World War II. Fascism's heyday ended with World War II, but it remained in some nations.

A. Communism in Russia

1. During World War I, the Russian czar abdicated in favor of a provisional republic, but the new government was unable to fix Russia's many economic and social problems and it chose to continue the czar's unpopular participation in World War I.

2. The Bolshevik wing of the Communist Party, led by Vladimir Lenin, ousted the provisional government from the capital and engaged in a bloody civil war against various groups, known as the "Whites" who opposed the communist "Reds."

3. The communists won and established the Union of Soviet Socialist Republics (USSR), but Lenin died shortly afterward, in 1924. Joseph Stalin emerged as the next leader and remained in power for almost 30 years. Until World War II, the USSR was shunned by the majority of the world community.

4. Starting in the late 1920s, Stalin implemented a series of Five Year Plans of government-directed economic and industrial growth. Under the Five Year Plans and their production goals, factories were built and massive public works programs, such as dam construction, were implemented. Stalin focused on heavy industry like steel and concrete production.

5. Stalin was a ruthless ruler who purged millions of his enemies, real and imagined.

   i. An estimated 14 million farmers and their families who resisted Stalin's plan to force them to work on collective farms were killed by execution or government-imposed starvation in the 1930s.

ii. *Gulags*—prison "reeducation camps"—sprang up throughout the Soviet Union, especially in Siberia. Little was known about these policies in the West. After Germany attacked Russia in 1941, Britain was eager to include Russia as an Allied power. Stalin relished his new role on the world stage, meeting with U.S. and British leaders to plan the war.

6. After World War II, the USSR emerged as a global power and began an aggressive campaign to spread communist influence. Rebellions against Soviet control in East Germany, Hungary, and Czechoslovakia in the three decades after World War II were met with brutal reprisals.

7. By the late twentieth century, signs of strain appeared in the Soviet system.

   i. The USSR's military rivaled that of the United States, but its economy proved inadequate at supplying consumer goods, unlike the economies of capitalist societies.

   ii. The economic pressures caused by global military interventions, notably in Afghanistan starting in 1979, overburdened the Soviet system.

   iii. In the early 1980s, U.S. President Ronald Reagan dramatically increased U.S. military spending, gambling that the Soviet leaders would choose to do the same and ignore growing discontent from their citizens who hoped for improved goods and services at home. Reagan guessed correctly.

8. In the mid-1980s, the Soviet Politburo—the policy-making council of the USSR—chose a leader who pledged to reform—but not end—the communist system: Mikhail Gorbachev.

   i. Gorbachev introduced limited capitalism (*perestroika*) and loosened restrictions on criticism of the government (*glasnost*). He hoped these measures, if doled out in a controlled fashion, would restore both the USSR's crumbling economy and people's faith in the communist system. They did neither. The world watched in amazement as former Soviet-controlled nations in eastern Europe—led by Poland's Solidarity movement—peacefully broke with communism in the late 1980s.

9. A 1991 military coup against Gorbachev failed, but soon after the coup, Gorbachev announced the dissolution of the USSR, and the Cold War ended. Russia then became—on paper at least—a capitalist-based democracy, but its future path remained murky.

B. Revolutions in China Lead to Communist Rule.

1. The Qing dynasty was overthrown in 1911 and was not replaced by a new imperial dynasty. This event marked the end of thousands of years of dynastic rule in China.

2. The new government was the Republic of China, promoted by Sun Yat-sen (Sun Yi Xian), a Western-educated member of the Chinese elite. Sun struggled to create a stable, unified China and sought aid from the West, but the only major nation to respond was the newly-formed Soviet Union. This support from communist sources had enormous long-term implications.

3. Sun died in 1925 and was replaced by Chiang Kai-Shek (Jiang Jieshí). Unlike Sun, Chiang vigorously opposed cooperation with communists. Regions in China fell into civil war between communists and "Nationalists" supporting the Republic. A major reason why many peasants supported the communists was their perception that the republic was both corrupt and inept.

4. When Japan invaded China in 1937, the communists and Nationalists united to fight their common enemy. When the United States entered World War II, China was added to the Allies, and Chiang met with U.S. and British leaders to plan war strategy.

5. At the end of World War II, China's civil war restarted and, in 1949, the communists, led by Mao Zedong, were victorious. The Nationalist government and millions of its supporters, backed by Western powers, fled to Taiwan and ruled from there.

6. Mao's government officially granted full legal and voting rights to women, which was a radical change from China's past. Many women served in high government positions. Unlike Lenin, who favored communist revolution by industrial workers in cities, Mao's main support came from agrarian peasants.

Test Tip

The AP World History exam has been known to ask about differences between Leninist and Maoist approaches to communist revolutions.

7. China supported communist North Korea in the Korean War by sending millions of soldiers into that conflict.

8. In the late 1950s, Mao pushed a *Great Leap Forward* that promoted industrial output over agricultural production. The result was an agrarian catastrophe that led to death by starvation for as many as 20 million people.

9. Mao's response to this disaster was to blame "outside" capitalist influences that he said were still prevalent in China, so a Cultural Revolution was enacted to purge all vestiges of Western culture. Widespread government persecutions and reeducation centers finally ended with Mao's death in 1976.

10. By the 1960s, two nations that might appear to be natural allies were enemies: the USSR and communist China. They fought over territories on their mutual borders and did little to support each other in spreading communism around the globe.

11. After Mao's death, reformers, including Deng Xiaoping, improved China's economy and its position on the world stage by inviting government-monitored capitalist

C. 1900 TO THE PRESENT

investment from the West. The economy and people's standard of living boomed into the early twenty-first century, but political reforms were slower to appear.

C. Fascism

1. Fascism was not limited to the Axis Powers of Germany, Italy, and Japan.

   i. Spain enacted fascism after a civil war in the 1930s, but it did not participate in expansion of territory like its European cohorts. Fascism ended in Spain in the mid-1970s.

   ii. In addition, governments in Argentina and Brazil incorporated elements of fascism in the 1940s and 1950s.

   iii. In all three countries, democratic movements replaced fascism by the 1980s.

 IV. Other Political Revolutions

A. Mexico

1. In Mexico, a revolution promising sweeping political, economic, and social reforms to promote the well-being of the masses began in 1910, and a constitution supporting those goals was adopted in 1917.

2. It was not until the 1930s, however, that land reform occurred. This involved taking millions of acres of land from large plantations held by foreign and domestic owners and giving it to peasant farmers.

3. Public education programs were enacted as well.

4. After World War II, the government allowed foreign interests to again buy land in Mexico, and the land reform program faded.

B. Iran

1. In the 1950s, a Western-backed emperor, the shah, was put into power in Iran. He supported foreign investment in his nation's oil industry and received military aid from the United States and Western Europe during the Cold War.

   i.   Iranian society allowed women to vote, and Western culture and education was encouraged.

   ii. In 1979, uprisings against government oppression of opponents forced the shah out of power.

2. The shah was replaced by a radical anti-Western Muslim leader, Ayatollah Khomeini. The ayatollah's message of Muslim unity, the supremacy of Islamic law over secular law, and rejection of Western influence was supported by many in Iran. Those who did not support the changes were brutally dealt with.

   i.   Women were required to be covered from head to toe, but they were still allowed to vote.

   ii. Khomeini actively pushed his brand of Islamic rule, promoting its spread throughout the Muslim world. He supplied rhetoric and money to support radical Islamic groups like Al-Qaeda throughout the Middle East, much to the dismay of the West.

Cold War Map

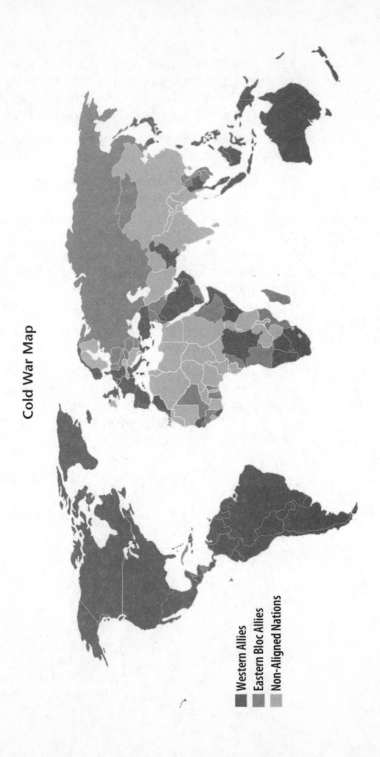

Western Allies

Eastern Bloc Allies

Non-Aligned Nations

Twentieth-Century Changes in Global Economics and Societies
c. 1900 to the Present

Test Tip

The writers of the AP World History exam are fond of asking multiple-choice and essay questions on the topic of globalism in the twentieth century.

I. The Promotion of Global Connections

A. Organizations Formed to Encourage Global Cooperation

1. The League of Nations and the United Nations were formed to promote international cooperation. Many other organizations formed for the same purpose.

   i. The Universal Postal Union and the International Telecommunication Union were founded in the late nineteenth century and were made part of the United Nations after World War II.

      ➤ Their job is to create agreements between and among member nations regarding exchanging international mail and communications, such as telephone, radio, and Internet usage.

2. The International Olympic Committee was also formed in the late nineteenth century. Its purpose was to promote international understanding through sports. The Olympics were canceled during the World Wars, but they continued to grow in popularity as the twentieth century progressed.

B. International Economic Organizations Formed

1. After World War II, several organizations promoted international trade and financial assistance to poorer nations and regions.

   i. The World Bank and the International Monetary Fund (IMF) promote sound banking principles and loan money to nations with developing economies.

   ii. The General Agreement on Tariffs and Trade (GATT) promoted international free trade. The World Trade Organization (WTO) replaced it in the late twentieth century.

2. The G7, founded in the 1970s, was an organization representing the interests of the world's seven largest economies. It has since become the G20.

   i. The communist version of these organizations was Comecon, founded by the USSR in the mid-twentieth century.

   ii. It disbanded after the fall of communism in Russia and the rest of Eastern Europe at the end of the twentieth century.

C. Regional Trade Agreements Developed

1. The European Union (EU).

   i. The EU was formed in the 1950s by six western European nations that wanted to lower trade barriers between and among themselves and create a common market to help compete against the giant U.S. economy that emerged after World War II.

   ii. Their original goal was to create a kind of "United States of Europe" with a common money system, a capital city, a flag, and a legislature. Its names over the years were the European Coal and Steel Community; then the European Economic Community; then the European Community; and finally, in 1993, the European Union.

   iii. In 1993, most of the twelve member nations from Western Europe went to a single monetary unit, the euro. England did not participate in that move. The capital of the EU is Brussels, Belgium; there is an EU flag and legislature and an EU passport.

iv. After the fall of communism in eastern Europe, the EU invited these European nations to join. By the early twenty-first century, 27 nations comprised the EU.

v. In its various forms, the EU oversaw a booming economy in the 1950s and 1960s, a major recession in the 1970s, and mild economic growth from the 1980s to the present.

2. In response to the success of the European Union, the United States, Mexico, and Canada entered into a free trade agreement called the North American Free Trade Agreement (NAFTA) in the early 1990s, but it did not include the political aspects of the EU's organization.

3. In 1960, oil-rich nations, primarily from the Middle East but also including members in Africa and South America, organized into a cartel, or trade union, that endeavored to regulate the global price of crude oil.

i. The cartel was named the Organization of Petroleum Exporting Countries (OPEC). OPEC became a household word in the West when its Arab members raised prices and reduced exports of oil to Western Europe and the United States after the 1973 Arab-Israeli War.

ii. The West supported Israel in that war, and many Arab leaders in OPEC pushed to punish Western Europe and the United States for that support. The combination of higher oil prices and reduced petroleum supplies had damaging effects on the West's economy. Inflation soared and unemployment went up. As a result, the West and the Arab world realized for the first time how dependent the West was on imported petroleum.

D. Multinational Corporations Abounded After World War II

1. In a trend that started in the nineteenth century, corporations that "went global" boomed along with the growth of the world's economy after World War II. Exxon,

McDonald's, General Motors, and Coca-Cola had their bases in the United States, but expanded to markets around the globe. Philips Electronics and Shell Oil Corporation based their international operations from headquarters in Europe. From East Asia, Sony Electronics, Toyota Motors, and Hyundai Motors shipped products around the world. Companies such as these were called multinational or transnational corporations.

E. Global Humanitarian Groups Sought to Respond to Human Suffering.

1. The oldest such group is the Red Cross, which was founded in England in the mid-nineteenth century. It is a private organization, but works with government agencies around the world. In majority-Muslim regions, it goes by the name Red Crescent.

2. Amnesty International raises awareness of the plight of political prisoners around the globe.

3. The World Health Organization is a UN agency committed to combating infectious diseases and promoting the general health of all citizens of the world.

4. UNICEF, also a UN agency, works for children's rights and their survival, development, and protection around the globe.

 Human Rights

A. After World War II, Ideas about Human Rights Gained Acceptance in Many Places.

1. The Nuremberg trials

   i. In 1945, the Allied Nations held trials for Nazi war criminals for crimes against humanity. These crimes referred to the torture and death campaigns that German government officials ordered, carried out, or consented to in their country and the countries they invaded. The Allied prosecutors charged the accused officials of violating basic human rights—a concept introduced during the Enlightenment. Those found guilty usually faced the death penalty.

2. Universal Declaration of Human Rights.

    i.   In 1948, the United Nations echoed the concepts from the Nuremberg Trials with its *Universal Declaration of Human Rights*.

    ii.   Among these rights are freedom of speech and religion; the right to life, liberty, and personal security; freedom of movement from another country or within a country; and the right to a fair trial, work, and education.

    iii.   While all member UN nations signed the declaration, not all fully participated in exercising its tenets.

3. Civil rights movements

    i.   In the 1950s and 1960s, African Americans pushed the U.S. government to fulfill its constitutional promises of equal rights for all. Dr. Martin Luther King, Jr., followed the nonviolent methods used in India by Mohandas Gandhi.

    ii.   Individuals in other nations began to call for additional rights as well.

    iii.   The most famous student protests occurred in Paris in 1968.

    iv.   Another civil rights movement was the lifting of apartheid in South Africa in the late twentieth century.

4. Women's rights

    i.   In the early twentieth century, Western adult women received voting rights in the United States and Britain.

    ii.   As part of the above-mentioned civil rights movement, women's groups in the United States, Europe, and Japan actively sought equal employment opportunities and social equality with men.

5. Despite civil rights gains made in Western cultures and increased governmental participation by women in communist nations such as China and the USSR, in many areas of the world human rights violations remained into the twenty-first century: children were forced into armies in Sudan, ethnic genocide killed almost 1 million people in and around Rwanda, and women were refused educational opportunities by the Taliban in Afghanistan—to list just a few examples.

B. Changes in Religions Had Global Effects.

1. Vatican II modernized the Roman Catholic Church.

   i. In the early 1960s, Pope John XXIII called for updates to the centuries-old traditions in the Roman Catholic Church. More participation by nonclergy in church services was encouraged, and the mass was no longer delivered in Latin but in the language of the local church. Pope John and his successors, most notably John Paul II, also promoted *ecumenism*, cooperation between faiths.

2. Eastern religions, particularly Buddhism, gained popularity in the West. Part of the reason for the spread of Eastern religions into the West may be the ecumenical spirit begun in the 1960s, and another might be the global popularity of the Beatles, who introduced aspects of South Asian music and faith to the West.

3. Religious revival in the West was brought on by the rising uncertainties that flowed through societies in the turbulent 1960s. One example of religious revival was the *Jesus movement* that involved millions of young people in Western culture.

4. Islam went through a conservative revival as well. Beginning in the 1950s, partly as a response against the growing influence of Western culture that came from contacts made in the oil trade, Islamic fundamentalism rejected the so-called decadent culture of the infidel West. Islamic fundamentalism's most famous examples were found in the Iranian Revolution and in the formation of terrorist groups such as *Al-Qaeda*.

C. Popular Culture and Global Consumerism.

1. The West was the center of the world's economy and had the most multinational corporations.

    i.   The United States specifically produced 50 percent of the world's products for most of the post–World War II era and had the means, through its global corporations, to distribute its goods around the world.

    ii. Cultural examples of this include U.S. clothing styles, music (like Elvis Presley or "The Twist" dance craze), movies, and television shows. This trend also flowed in the opposite direction. For example, the Beatles, who were from Britain, were even more popular around the world than Elvis. *Bollywood*, the nickname for India's film industry, which originated in Bombay (today's Mumbai), produced more films than Hollywood and became popular in the West.

2. Sports became a global phenomenon.

    i.   World Cup soccer was a passion for individuals and nations around the world.

    ii. U.S. sports, such as baseball and basketball, had many participants and fans in Europe and Asia, so much so that, by the end of the decade, European and Asian professional athletes were playing for teams in the United States.

PART III

KEY CONCEPTS
and Themes

Art, Architecture, and Literature Review

The chapters in Part II, "Chronological Review," included several important references to literature, government documents, art, and architecture. Below is a handy table that contains important trends in art and architecture and essential examples of writings in world history.

PRE-HISTORY TO c. 600 B.C.E.

ART	ARCHITECTURE	LITERATURE/ DOCUMENTS
Cave paintings— found globally		
Religious figurines— found globally		
Statuary— Mesopotamia, Egypt, Greece	Sun-dried bricks, the arch, ziggurats (religious temples), Assyrian bas reliefs— Mesopotamia	*Epic of Gilgamesh* and the *Code of Hammurabi*— Mesopotamia
Writing systems— Mesopotamia, Phoenicia, Egypt, China, India	Pyramids—Egypt	*Book of the Dead*—Egypt
Bronze figurines— China	Cities—Babylon (Mesopotamia), Memphis (Egypt), Catal-huyuk (Turkey), Mohenjo-Daro (India), Zhengzhou (China), Caral (Peru)	Hebrew Scriptures— Eastern Mediterranean
Large stone heads— Mesoamerica	Stonehenge monoliths— England	*Upanishads*— South Asia

c. 600 B.C.E.–c. 600 C.E.

ART	ARCHITECTURE	LITERATURE/ DOCUMENTS
Increased realism in Greek and Roman statuary— Mediterranean	"Classical" Greek and Roman temples— Mediterranean	Greek philosophy, plays, scientific journals, *History of the Persian Wars*. Roman *Twelve Tables*— Mediterranean
Mosaics— Byzantine (Eastern Mediterranean)	Hellenistic buildings— Southwest, Central and South Asia, North Africa	*Code of Justinian*— Byzantine (Eastern Mediterranean)
Christian iconography— Mediterranean		Hindu *Bhagavad Gita*
Nazca lines—Peru	Moche buildings— Peru	*New Testament*, writings of Augustine— Mediterranean Buddhist *Four Noble Truths* and *Eight-Fold Path*—India
Terracotta army— China	Buddhist temples and statues—South, Southeast, and East Asia (some aspects of Hellenism)	Confucian *Analects*; Daoist *Daodejing*— China
Landscape paintings— China	Hindu temples and statuary—South Asia	

c. 600–c. 1450

ART	ARCHITECTURE	LITERATURE/ DOCUMENTS
Continued Christian iconography— Europe and Byzantine	Gothic cathedrals— Europe; Hagia Sofia— Byzantine church (Turkey) Rock churches— Ethiopia	Journals from Marco Polo and Ibn Battuta (Italy and North Africa, respectively)
Islamic imagery of Muhammad—North Africa to South Asia	Mosques, minarets, courtyard complexes—North Africa to South Asia	The *Qur'an*, "Arabic" numerals, calligraphy, Muslim science journals, Ibn Khaldun's histories, *1001 Nights*—Southwest Asia, North Africa
	Mayan temples (for example, Tikal) and statuary— Mesoamerica Inca stone walls; Machu Picchu—Peru	
Tang–Song ceramics—China		Block printing—China
	Angkor Wat temple complex—Southeast Asia	*Pillow Book* and *Tale of Genji*—Japan
		Epic of Sundiata—Mali
	Great Zimbabwe— Southeast Africa	

c. 1450–c. 1750

ART	ARCHITECTURE	LITERATURE/ DOCUMENTS
Renaissance Revival of Greco/Roman art styles—Europe	European influences in Latin American buildings	Moveable type printing press— Europe Copernicus's heliocentric theory published—Europe
African figurines become popular in Europe	Baroque architecture— Western Europe Western European-style buildings in St. Petersburg, Russia	Martin Luther's *95 Theses,* Treaty of Tordesillas, writings by Shakespeare, *Two Treatises on Government* and other writings of the Enlightenment— Europe
	Taj Mahal—India	Block printing—Japan
Aztec and Inca paintings that depict the Spanish conquest		

c. 1750–c. 1900

ART	ARCHITECTURE	LITERATURE/ DOCUMENTS
Romanticism (ex. by David), Realism (ex. Courbet), Impressionism (ex. Van Gogh) —Europe	Neo-Classicalism— Europe, the United States Brick and steel skyscrapers—Europe, the United States	*Declaration of Independence, Declaration of Sentiments,* Monroe Doctrine, Gettysburg Address—the United States
		Declaration of the Rights of Man and of the Citizen—France Fiction by Dickens, *A Vindication of the Rights of Woman, On the Origin of Species, Communist Manifesto*—England
		Emancipation of the Peasants from Serfdom— Russia
		Treaty of Nanjing (Opium Wars)—China, England *Letter to Queen Victoria*— China
		Jamaica Letter—Latin America
	Western-influenced building styles— South, East and Southeast Asia, Africa	Tanzimat Constitution, Ottoman Empire; Meiji Constitution, Japan

1900 TO THE PRESENT

ART	ARCHITECTURE	LITERATURE/ DOCUMENTS
Cubism, Abstract art, Dadaism— Europe, the United States *Guernica*—Europe	Bauhaus style— Europe Glass and steel skyscrapers—Europe, the United States, East Asia, Southeast Asia	Fourteen Points—the United States and Europe Treaty of Versailles, *All Quiet on the Western Front, Mein Kampf, Documents of Vatican II,* Maastricht Treaty—Europe
Propaganda posters for World Wars I and II— Global	Prairie school style— the United States	*Three Principles of the People, Quotations from Chairman Mao*—China
Socialist Realism —USSR, China		*What Is to Be Done?*— Russia
		Writings by Gandhi—India
		Universal Declaration of Human Rights—United Nations
		Writings by Martin Luther King, Jr.; *The Feminine Mystique*—the United States

Nineteen Key Concepts
in AP World History

By now, you know that AP World History is about keeping the big picture in mind at all times. The AP World History curriculum framework helps you do that by providing nineteen key concepts for world history. These concepts were covered in more detail in Part II, "Chronological Review," but in keeping with our big-picture theme, they are provided here in shorter form. Each historical period has only three or four key concepts.

As you review the key concepts, recall the specific information you've already studied in Chapters 2 through 20. For example, look at Period 1, Key Concept 1.1 below, and write down specific terms that come to mind when you read that key concept. Next, look back at Chapters 2 and 3 and see how you did. Repeat this process for all nineteen key concepts and you'll be another step closer to AP World History success.

PERIOD 1: TECHNOLOGICAL AND ENVIRONMENTAL TRANSFORMATIONS, to c. 600 B.C.E.

Key Concept 1.1: Big Geography and the Peopling of the Earth

Key Concept 1.2: The Neolithic Revolution and Early Agricultural Societies

Key Concept 1.3: The Development and Interactions of Early Agricultural, Pastoral, and Urban Societies

PERIOD 2: ORGANIZATION AND REORGANIZATION OF HUMAN SOCIETIES, c. 600 B.C.E. to c. 600 C.E.

Key Concept 2.1: The Development and Codification of Religious and Cultural Traditions

Key Concept 2.2: The Development of States and Empires

Key Concept 2.3: Emergence of Interregional Networks of Communication and Exchange

PERIOD 3: REGIONAL AND INTERREGIONAL INTER-ACTIONS, c. 600 C.E. to c. 1450 C.E.

Key Concept 3.1: Expansion and Intensification of Communication and Exchange Networks

Key Concept 3.2: Continuity and Innovation of State Forms and Their Interactions

Key Concept 3.3: Increased Economic Productive Capacity and Its Consequences

PERIOD 4: GLOBAL INTERACTIONS, c. 1450 to c. 1750

Key Concept 4.1: Globalizing Networks of Communication and Exchange

Key Concept 4.2: New Forms of Social Organization and Modes of Production

Key Concept 4.3: State Consolidation and Imperial Expansion

PERIOD 5: INDUSTRIALIZATION AND GLOBAL INTEGRATION, c. 1750 to c. 1900

Key Concept 5.1: Industrialization and Global Capitalism

Key Concept 5.2: Imperialism and Nation-State Formation

Key Concept 5.3: Nationalism, Revolution, and Reform

Key Concept 5.4: Global Migration

PERIOD 6: ACCELERATING GLOBAL CHANGE AND REALIGNMENTS, c. 1900 to the Present

KEY CONCEPTS AND THEMES

Thinking Skills, Themes, and Historiography

The AP World History course is organized to help you prepare for success on the exam. The exam creators understand very well how difficult studying 10,000 years of history can be, so they have categorized historical skills and content into manageable groups. The well-prepared AP World History student will begin to see the big picture of history after studying these must-know skills and themes.

I. Historical Thinking Skills

The historical thinking skills are: (1) analyzing historical sources and evidence; (2) making historical connections; (3) chronological reasoning; and (4) creating and supporting a historical argument. These skills are not only useful in writing history essays and the short-answer questions, but also with choosing the right answers to multiple-choice questions on the AP World History exam. Find tips for addressing the historical thinking skills in the chapters in Part IV of this book, Test-Taking Strategies.

A. Analyzing Historical Sources and Evidence

This is a skill in which you use historical evidence (i.e., historical documents) to craft a thesis and develop an essay. This skill has document-based question (DBQ) written all over it, but it can also help you with the multiple-choice questions that contain art, photos, and charts. Understanding the point of view of a document and its historical context is important.

B. Making Historical Connections

1. In multiple-choice questions you may be asked to analyze similarities and differences among and between civilizations or to place a choice in the correct historical context.

2. On the short-answer questions, the long essay questions, or the DBQ, you may be asked to connect specific events to broader processes on a regional or global scale (contextualization). For example, Arab nationalism in the twentieth century was just one part of global nationalist trends in that era. Or you may be asked to write a compare-and-contrast essay or a synthesis essay.

C. Chronological Reasoning

You may be asked to apply this historical skill in the multiple-choice, short-answer or essay questions about periodization (knowing roughly when things happened), causes and effects of major events, or continuities and changes over time.

D. Creating and Supporting a Historical Argument

You have no doubt figured out that this skill will be applied predominantly in the DBQ and long-essay section of the exam. In chapter 29, you will learn how to create a workable thesis, incorporate historical examples and frame an argument into a cohesive essay.

II. **Five Thematic Learning Objectives in AP World History**

As you study these overarching themes that weave in and out of all of world history, recall specific examples that you've learned from Part II, "Chronological Review," in this book. When you can provide specific answers to each of the overarching thematic questions below, you will be on the road to success.

A. Interaction Between Humans and the Environment

This theme addresses how humans have shaped the environment and vice-versa. For example, migrating humans tend to travel through mountain passes, not over mountains. Be prepared to address these overarching questions: (1) How have people used tools and technologies to adapt to and affect the environment? (2) How has human migration and settlement been influenced by the environment? (3) How has the environment changed because of human population growth and urbanization? (4) How have industrialization and expanding global connections interacted with the environment?

B. Development and Interaction of Cultures

As you might expect, this theme covers religions and philosophies, ideologies, the arts and technology. Patriarchy in its different forms is addressed here as well. Overarching questions for you to focus on include: (1) How and why have religions, philosophies, and ideologies developed and changed as they spread? (2) How have religions, philosophies, and ideologies affected societies over time? (3) How were technologies adapted and transformed as they spread? (4) How do the arts reflect specific societies?

C. State-building, Expansion, and Conflict

It should come as no surprise that this theme is about governments and what they do, including the roles of rulers, their interactions with their subjects, diplomacy and war, trade, and causes and consequences of their rise and fall. Overarching questions for this theme include: (1) How have different kinds of governments developed over time? (2) How have governments interacted with economies, societies, cultures and the environment? (3) How have trade, war and alliances influenced the building, expansion, and fall of governments?

D. Creation, Expansion, and Interaction of Economic Systems

This theme studies the ways that humans have produced, distributed, and consumed goods and services across time and place. Exchanges of trade goods across various webs of connections is a favorite topic on AP World History essays. Overarching questions about economics include: (1) How and to what extent have methods of production and exchange

KEY CONCEPTS AND THEMES

changed over time? (2) How have labor systems developed and changed over time? (3) How have economic systems and their ideologies and institutions influenced each other over time? (4) What relationships developed among local, regional, and global economic systems over time?

E. Development and Transformation of Social Structures

This theme is about relationships between humans: Roles within families, gender, race, and attitudes about their place in society. Overarching questions about society include: (1) How have distinctions based on families, ethnicity, class, gender, and race influenced development of and changes in social hierarchies, i.e., who is on the top and who is on the bottom? (2) In what ways have social categories, roles, and practices stayed the same and changed over time? (3) How have political, economic, cultural, and demographic changes affected social hierarchies over time?

III. Historiography

Historiography is the study of . . . history. In other words, how do different historians view the past? Sometimes political preferences color an historian's view of the past. As another example, historians can't help but view the past through the lens of the times they live in. For example, it wasn't long ago that Western historians thought the Mongols were an "unstoppable and bloody tide of horror," but more recently, many have come to see the Mongols as "agents of change" who exchanged technology, allowed religious free-dom, and established the *Pax Mongolica*—the Mongol peace that developed with their empire. Still another example that you may have discussed in your World History class is the debates histori-ans have had over the years—both positive and negative—about Columbus's legacy. The AP World History exam will have ques-tions (particularly in the multiple-choice section) about historians' diverse views of the past.

Important Periodization
in AP World History

History isn't like math, where 1 + 1 equals 2 no matter what. Instead, history is kind of squishy, offering different points of view concerning the past. *Periodization* is the way historians divide the past into eras to help people organize events and civilizations into manageable chunks of time. The bottom line is, you need to know when things happened. Not exact dates, but which things happened in which eras. Some students who learn history only by themes think that Confucius, Buddha, Jesus, and Muhammad all lived at the same time.

You also need to know that not everything happens at the same time around the world. The Industrial Revolution, which the West has experienced for 200 years, has not yet spread everywhere. Knowledge of "uneven history," as shown in the examples below, is key to understanding what makes AP World History unique.

Below are the standard dates set for AP World History periods, followed by some alternate dates that historians have suggested for each era.

PERIOD 1 Pre-History: to c. 600 BCE

c. 8000 BCE: standard date for the beginning of the Neolithic Revolution (agriculture) in Mesopotamia.

But agriculture developed at other times in other places:

c. 7000 BCE: agriculture developed in East Asia

c. 6000 BCE: agriculture developed in the Nile region

c. 3000 BCE: agriculture developed in Andean South America

PERIOD 2: c. 600 BCE–c. 600 CE, the Classical Era

But the following dates define the Classical Era in these regions:

    c. 800 BCE: the rise of Greek city-states

    c. 320 BCE: the rise of the Mauryan dynasty

    c. 250 CE: beginning of Mesoamerican Classical Era

PERIOD 3: c. 600 CE to c.1450 CE, the Post-Classical Era

But these dates might also define the beginning of the period:

    c. 220 CE: the Han Dynasty ended

    c. 476 CE: the Western Roman Empire ended

    c. 550 CE: the Gupta Empire ended

    c. 608 CE: the Tang Dynasty began

    c. 622 CE: Islam introduced

PERIOD 4: c. 1450–c. 1750, the Early Modern Era

But these dates could also work as the beginning of the period:

    c. 1433: Zheng He's voyages of exploration ended

    c. 1440: the printing press developed in Europe

    1453: the Ottomans took control of Constantinople

    1492: Columbus reached the Americas

PERIOD 5: c. 1750–c.1900, the Early Industrial Era

But these dates might also mark the beginning of the period:

    c. 1730: beginnings of the Industrial Revolution in Europe

    1757: the Battle of Plassey began English colonization in India

1775: the start of the American Revolution

1789: the start of the French Revolution

1791: the start of the Haitian Revolution

PERIOD 6: c. 1900 to the Present

You might think it's hard to argue about when the twentieth century began, but historians will do it. Maybe they just like to argue. Anyway, consider these alternatives:

1789–1914: is referred to by some Western historians as the "long nineteenth century"

1914: the start of World War I

1917: the communist revolution in Russia

This exercise got you to think, didn't it? Aha! Now you're doing an important historical skill.

KEY CONCEPTS AND THEMES

Important Civilizations, Empires, and Dynasties

In each of the six chronological eras, some civilizations are featured more than others on the AP World History exam. On the next two pages are the "all-stars" of each era, arranged by their geographic region of influence. As you study, note particularly the civilizations that cross multiple time periods and/or geographic regions.

Civilizations of Influence in Specific Time Periods

Geographical Region	To c. 600 BCE	c. 600 BCE to c. 600 CE	c. 600 CE to c. 1450 CE
Southwest Asia	Mesopotamia, Persia	Hellenism, Parthian	Abbasid, Ottoman, Mongols
West Africa			Ghana
East Africa	Bantus	Bantus	Ethiopia, Zimbabwe, Swahili States
North Africa	Egypt, Kush	Hellenism	Arab, Ottoman
Mediterranean		Greek, Roman ("Mediterranean Civilization")	Byzantine
South Asia	Indus Valley	Mauryan, Gupta	Delhi Sultanates
East Asia	Shang	Qin, Han	Tang, Song, Mongol (Yuan), Ming
Central Asia		Persian	Mongols
Americas	Olmec, Chavin	Mayan, Teotihuacan, Moche	Maya, Aztec
Europe			Muslim Iberia (Portugal and Spain)

c. 1450 to c. 1750	c. 1750 to c. 1900	c. 1900 to the present
Ottoman, Safavid	Ottoman	Ottoman, England, France, Israel, Iran, Iraq, Saudi Arabia, Turkey
Songhay	Influence from Western Europe	
Ethiopia	Ethiopia, Influence from Western Europe	Influence from Western Europe
Arab, Ottoman	Influence from Western Europe	Algeria, Egypt
Ottoman	Ottoman	
Mughal	British Raj	India, Pakistan
Ming, Qing (Manchu), Tokugawa Shogunate	Qing (Manchu), Meiji, European "spheres of influence"	China, Japan, Korea, "Asian Tigers"
Mughals		
Aztec, Inca, influence from Western Europe	United States, Mexico, Haiti, Brazil	United States, Mexico, Cuba, Panama
Portugal, Spain, France, England, Holland, Holy Roman Empire, Russia	Western Europe, Russia	Axis Powers, Allies, North Atlantic Treaty Organization (NATO), Warsaw Pact, European Union

Important Migrations and Trade Routes

On the AP World History exam, it is important to know the movement of people (migration) and trade networks over time. Study the outline below of a few examples of migration and trade patterns, and make connections to what you learned in Part II about the political, social, and economic causes and effects of migration and of trade.

I. Migrations

A. To c. 600 BCE

➤ Southeast Asians across the Pacific (Oceania)

➤ East Asians to North America continuing to South America

➤ Central Asians into India, Europe (Indo-Europeans)

➤ Central Africans to eastern and southern Africa (Bantus)

B. c. 600 BCE–c. 600 CE

➤ Central Asia into Europe (Huns)

➤ Germanic peoples within Europe (e.g., Goths and Vandals)

➤ Continued Bantu migration

C. c. 600–c. 1450

➤ Vikings from northern Europe into France, Russia, Iceland, and Greenland

➤ Mongols south and west across Asia and into eastern Europe

➤ Arabs across North Africa and into Spain

D. c. 1450–c. 1750

➤ Europeans to the Americas

➤ Africans into Southwest Asia, Europe, and the Americas

E. c. 1750–c. 1900

➤ Europeans to the Americas

➤ South Asians and East Asians to the Americas, Southeast Asia, and Oceania

F. c. 1900 to the present

➤ South and Central Americans to North America

➤ Migrations between India and Pakistan after the Partition

➤ Africans into Europe

➤ South Asians into the Middle East

II. Trade Areas and Terms

The AP World History exam requires knowledge about trade regions and what was exchanged in those regions over time. Study the merchandise, religions, diseases, and technologies in the outline below. "Must-know" features are included at the bottom of each time frame.

A. To c. 600 BCE

➤ *Important trade regions:* limited regional trade in all areas

➤ *Must-know terms involving trade:* barter systems, weapons, belief systems

B. c. 600 BCE–c. 600 CE

➤ *Important trade regions:*

• Silk Roads

• Indian Ocean

- Mediterranean
- Trans-Sahara

➤ *Must-know terms involving trade:* cities along trade routes, Han/Rome trade network, caravans, *dhows*, decline of trade cities, lateen sails, monsoon winds, oasis, camels, spread of Christianity and Buddhism

C. c. 600 CE–c. 1450

➤ *Important trade regions:*

- Silk Roads
- Indian Ocean
- South China Sea
- Mediterranean
- Trans-Sahara
- Black Sea
- Mesoamerica
- Andes

➤ *Must-know terms involving trade:* Ibn Battuta, Marco Polo, Pax Mongolica, Black Death, Straits of Malacca, spread of Islam, Dar al-Islam, Mansa Musa, Zheng He, "china" (porcelain), revival of trade cities

D. c. 1450–c. 1750

➤ *Important trade areas:*

- Atlantic World
- Indian Ocean
- South China Sea
- Russia

➤ *Must-know terms:* Columbian Exchange, global trade network, African slave trade, mercantilism, Potosi, British raj, Russian fur trade, silver, black ships (Japan)

E. c. 1750–c. 1900

➤ *Important trade areas:*

- Europe to its colonies in Africa and Asia

- Atlantic World

- Russia

- Suez Canal

➤ *Must-know terms:* industrialization, imperialism, capitalism, Marxism, trade unions, steam ships, trains, Opium Wars, spheres of influence, Meiji Restoration, open-door policy

F. c. 1900 to the present

➤ *Important trade areas:*

- Panama Canal

- Pacific Rim

- Persian Gulf

- the Internet

➤ *Must-know terms:* Great Depression, fascism, communism, OPEC, U.S. economic power, coca-colonialism, European Union, NAFTA, free trade, World Bank, World Trade Organization, multinational/transnational corporations, Asian Tigers, China

Important Technology
in AP World History

"When did people start using *that*?" It depends on where the people were at the time. You know from your class study that *technology*—making and using tools to change the natural state of the environment—isn't an instant global event. The list below highlights major technological developments and the first known places they occurred. Some came along at later times, independently, and in different regions. Many ideas spread along trade routes from their places of origin. As you review this list after studying the historical review in Part II, consider the effects these inventions had on societies.

BEGINNINGS OF CIVILIZATIONS TO c. 600 BCE

Domestication of animals, agriculture, irrigation, dams, wheel, plow, the sail, metalwork, brick-making, the arch, cities, governments, geometry, algebra, writing, calendars: early developments in Mesopotamia, Egypt, and China

c. 600 BCE–c. 600 CE

➤ Coins: Persia

➤ "Arabic" numerals: South Asia

➤ Compass, wood pulp paper, porcelain, canals, horse collar, stirrup: China

➤ Astrolabe, lateen sail, concrete, crop rotation: China and South Asia

c. 600 CE–c. 1450

➤ Paper money, block printing, gunpowder, firearms: China

➤ Mechanical clock, eyeglasses, English longbow, wheeled plow: Europe

➤ University system of education: North Africa

c. 1450–c. 1750

➤ Alphabetic, moveable-type printing press; telescope; microscope; steam engine; factory textile machines: Europe

c. 1750–c. 1900

➤ Steamboat, steam locomotive, steel ships, steel-framed skyscrapers, machine gun, light bulb, telephone, radio, typewriter, movie projector, electric and gasoline motors, cotton gin, sewing machine, steel plow, mechanical reaper, automobile: Europe and the United States

c. 1900 TO THE PRESENT

➤ Airplane, liquid-fuel rocket, communications satellite, nuclear power, television, transistor, electronic computer, the Internet, penicillin, electronic medical imaging: the United States and Europe

PART IV
TEST-TAKING
Strategies

Strategies for the Multiple-Choice Questions

The AP World History exam begins with a 55-question, 55-minute multiple-choice section. Although the AP World History curriculum guide says that the course runs "to the present," the reality is that the exam creators know that most teachers and professors won't get much past the end of the Cold War in the late 1980s, so they don't tend to ask many questions beyond that date. But a quick review of highlights of the post–Cold War era can't hurt, if you have the time.

In addition, if you look at the early chapters of this book, you'll see that the exam questions are divided into six time frames. The first, "Beginnings to c. 600 BCE," accounts for only 5 percent of the exam. Do the math: 5 percent of 55 questions is 2.75 questions, so there will likely be only 3 or so multiple-choice questions from that era. The next era, c. 600 BCE–c. 600 CE, is covered in 15 percent of the exam, or roughly 8 multiple-choice questions. Each of the other time periods covers about 20 percent of the exam, or about 11 multiple-choice questions per era.

Some multiple-choice questions are comparative. That is, they ask you to compare societies in different time periods. It's important to understand that the AP World History exam is all about comparisons across time and place—getting the big picture and making connections. Many multiple-choice questions will involve only one time period. Some multiple-choice questions will feel like "gimmes" and others will be brain-rattling hard. That's to be expected. Hardly anyone ever gets all the multiple-choice questions right, so even if you miss 15 or so, you're living large. Hey, even if you miss *half* the multiple-choice questions, you still have a good chance of earning a 3—if you do okay on the essays.

What you *won't* find on the AP World History exam are "recall" multiple-choice questions. Here's an example:

The Tang Empire was in

(A) China

(B) Mesoamerica

(C) India

(D) Europe

By the way, the answer is (A). Instead, what you will find are sets of 2 to 5 questions that are anchored to some type of stimulus, like a document, chart, map, or art.

To answer 55 questions in 55 minutes means you get 60 seconds to answer each question. Math is so easy! Since the questions come in sets attached to a stimulus, you might have as much as 5 minutes to read the stimulus and answer the 5 accompanying questions. That might not sound like a lot of time, but with practice, you'll find it is.

The best way to deal with fears of running out of time is to first answer all the multiple-choice questions that seem easy to you. When you get to the end of the multiple-choice section, go back and spend time on the ones you didn't get on the first run-through.

Test Tip

Keep in mind, especially if you or your teacher use multiple-choice questions from previous exams or older exam study guides for practice, that the number of questions and the multiple-choice format changed starting with the 2017 exam.

The multiple-choice questions generally run in chronological order from question 1 to about question 27. That means the first questions will come from the earliest time periods and continue chronologically "to the present" until around question 27. Then, the questions "reset" back to the earliest time periods and continue chronologically again until number 55.

Answer all of the questions. Don't skip even one. If you don't have any idea, guess. Even if you have 10 questions to go and 30 seconds left, bubble in those circles on the answer sheet. You have a 25% chance of getting each guess right and that's a lot better than skipping a question and having a 0% chance.

Don't be discouraged if you "feel" like you missed a lot of multiple-choice questions. You can miss about half of them and still be in the "3" range headed into your short answer and essay questions.

PRACTICE MULTIPLE-CHOICE QUESTIONS

Use the excerpt below and your knowledge of world history to answer questions 1–3.

> I am the LORD your God.
> You shall have no other gods.
> You shall create no images or likenesses of Me.
> You shall not take the LORD's name in vain.
> Remember the Sabbath day.
> Honor your father and mother.
> Do not kill.
> Do not commit adultery.
> Do not steal.
> Do not bear false witness.
> Do not take your neighbor's wife.
> Do not take your neighbor's goods.

> —Hebrew law, Southwest Asia,
> c. 15th century BCE

1. Which of the following best marks a similarity between these Hebrew laws and other legal codes from the Mediterranean region in the era before c. 600 BCE?

    (A) They were all based on the Code of Hammurabi.

    (B) They all featured legal and moral codes of conduct.

    (C) They were all written in stone.

    (D) They were all created by leaders of empires.

    The correct answer is (B). Legal codes from the Mediterranean region included both legal and moral codes of conduct. Egyptian law codes were not influenced by Hammurabi's code (A); not all were written in stone—Egyptians wrote on papyrus (C); and the Hebrew Ten Commandments were not created by an emperor because they had not yet formed an empire.

2. How did the Hebrew faith differ from other religions of the Mediterranean region?

    (A) Only the Hebrew faith claimed that their laws were created by a deity.

    (B) Only the Hebrew faith outlawed lying (bearing false witness).

    (C) Only the Hebrew faith was monotheistic.

    (D) Only the Hebrew faith had no clear founder.

    The correct answer is (C). Only the Hebrew faith was monotheistic. Most early law codes claimed authority from a deity (or deities) (A) and most made bearing false witness a crime (B). Hinduism has no clear founder (D).

3. Historians have noted similarities between some Hebrew laws and other legal codes found in Southwest Asia. What best explains these similarities?

   (A) They were under the same government when their laws were created.

   (B) Other legal codes probably took their concepts from Hebrew laws.

   (C) All of Southwest Asia followed the same religion in the era before c. 600 BCE.

   (D) The Hebrew law codes borrowed concepts from other law codes in the region.

The correct answer is (D). The Hebrew law codes borrowed concepts from other law codes in the region. For example, some parts of Hebraic law contain clear inspiration from Babylon's Code of Hammurabi. When the Hebrews wrote the Ten Commandments, they were not under the control of an outside empire (A). There is no evidence to support choice (B). Southwest Asia had many varied religions in the era before c. 600 BCE (C).

Use the excerpt below and your knowledge of world history to answer questions 4–6.

> If a husband be unworthy, then he possesses nothing by which to control his wife. If a wife be unworthy, then she possesses nothing with which to serve her husband. If a husband does not control his wife, then the rules of conduct concerning his authority are abandoned and broken. If a wife does not serve her husband, when the proper relationship between men and women and the natural order of things are neglected and destroyed. As a matter of fact the purpose of controlling of women by men, and the serving of men by women is the same.
>
> —Ban Zhao, elite woman of the Han Dynasty,
> late first century CE

4. The system of social mores that Ban Zhao comments on is based on

   (A) Confucianism

   (B) Legalism

   (C) Zoroastrianism

   (D) Buddhism

The correct answer is (A). The codes of behavior written by Confucius inform these concepts. Legalism was the political philosophy under the Qin Dynasty (B). Zoroastrianism was a religion originating in Persia (C). Buddhism entered China from India, but was a religion that did not subjugate women to the extent that Confucianism did.

5. In China, the ruling families, such as those that led the Han Dynasty, maintained their authority so long as

    (A) they obeyed the laws in the Twelve Tables.

    (B) they held the Mandate of Heaven.

    (C) the army supported them through the Daimyo system.

    (D) the voters elected them to office.

The correct answer is (B). The Twelve Tables was the basis of the legal system in the Roman legal system (A). The Daimyo system involved feudal lords in Japan (C). Chinese emperors were not elected to office (D).

6. In what way did the effects of the fall of the Han Dynasty compare with the fall of the Roman Empire?

    (A) The Roman empire faced invasion from outside nomadic groups; the Han Dynasty managed to keep nomadic groups out.

    (B) Both the Han and Roman empires quickly rebuilt their political and social structures after they fell.

    (C) Neither the Han nor the Roman empire experienced a drop in population due to widespread diseases.

    (D) The Han Dynasty fell, but social order was maintained; the Roman Empire fell and most social order collapsed.

The correct answer is (D). The Han Dynasty did not keep nomadic groups out (A). The Romans did not quickly rebuild their political and social structures (B). Both empires experienced a drop in population due to widespread diseases (C).

Use the excerpt below and your knowledge of world history to answer questions 7–9.

> The city of Ghana [in West Africa] consists of two towns lying on a plain, one of which is inhabited by Muslims and is large, possessing twelve mosques, each has its Imam and paid reciters of the Quran. The town possesses a large number of learned men. The other town is inhabited by the king. His residence consists of a palace and a number of dome-shaped dwellings, surrounded by a city wall. In the town is a mosque, where Muslims on diplomatic missions come to hear the king pray. The town where the king lives is surrounded by domed huts where priest-magicians live; in the nearby woods are the religious idols and tombs of the kings. Special guards protect this area and prevent anyone from entering it so that no foreigners know what is inside.
>
> —Al-Bakri, 11th century Muslim geographer
> and historian from Spain (Al-Andalus)

7. Al-Bakri describes a culture that blends traditions from different belief systems. World historians call this and similar blending of traditions

    (A) syncretism

    (B) global migration

    (C) nationalism

    (D) theocracy

The correct answer is (A). World historians call this and similar blending of tradition syncretism. *Global migration* involves the moving of people, but not necessarily the blending of their cultures (B). *Nationalism* is pride in one's country and/or cultural heritage (C). *Theocracy* is government run under religious guidelines (D).

8. West Africa saw a blending of Islam with local traditional beliefs. Which of these is the clearest example of another such religious blending?

   (A) Hinduism in India

   (B) Judaism in Southwest Asia

   (C) Catholicism in Latin America

   (D) Shamanism in the Northwest Americas

The correct answer is (C). Catholicism in Latin America also featured syncretism with indigenous beliefs (such as the Virgin of Guadeloupe). Hinduism largely stayed in India (A). Judaism incorporated very little from nearby religions (B), especially compared to Catholicism. The same is also true with Shamanism in the Northwest Americas (D).

9. What factor best explains why a person from Spain could travel to and move about freely in Ghana?

   (A) The leader of Ghana invited tourists to explore his land.

   (B) Al-Bakri was sent as a missionary by the leader of his monastery.

   (C) Ghana was a colony of Spain in the 11th century.

   (D) Al-Bakri shared a common religious faith with the leader of Ghana.

The correct answer is (D). Choices (A), (B), and (C) are historically inaccurate explanations.

Use the image below and your knowledge of world history to answer questions 10–12.

(1885 newspaper cartoon by American Thomas Nast titled, "The World's Plunderers. Germany, England and Russia grab what they can of Africa and Asia." The left figure holds a sack that reads "German Grab-Bag"; the middle figure, "British Grab-Bag"; the right figure, "Russian Grab-Bag")

10. The cartoon above reflects what 19th century global process?

   (A) The provisions of the treaty that ended the Opium Wars

   (B) European imperialism

   (C) The Industrial Revolution

   (D) The rise of Marxism

The correct answer is (B). The Opium Wars focused on a trade dispute between China and Britain (A). The Industrial Revolution and the rise of Marxism are not the focus of the cartoon (C, D).

11. Which of these was a principal factor that led to the 19th century global process depicted in the cartoon?

    (A) Trade agreements between Germany, Britain, and Russia

    (B) Military alliances with Germany, Britain, and Russia on one side, and Africa and Asia on the other

    (C) The development of new transportation and medical technologies

    (D) African and Asian demands for products from Europe

The correct answer is (C). Steamboats, trains, and improved medicines made the "new" imperialism of the 19th century into previously uncolonized regions possible. The cartoon does not refer to trade agreements (A) or military alliances (B). The opposite was true for (D).

12. The Berlin Conference of 1885 had which of the following as a principal goal?

    (A) promote free trade among European nations

    (B) provide assistance for new nations such as Germany and Italy

    (C) establish international time zones

    (D) negotiate the European division of African colonies

The correct answer is (D). Promoting free trade among European nations began in the 1950s with the European Coal and Steel Community (later the European Union) (A). No assistance was provided by other European countries for new nations, such as Germany and Italy (B). International time zones were established by the International Meridian Conference in 1884 (C).

Use the image below and your knowledge of world history to answer questions 13–15.

—Cartoon by Illingworth, British "Daily Mail" newspaper, 1947

13. The cartoon above is best understood in the context of

   (A) the Russian-German Non-Aggression pact during World War II.

   (B) free trade agreements between Eastern and Western Europe in the mid-20th century.

   (C) the growing popularity of Eastern European artistic styles in the post-World War II era.

   (D) Western European concerns about Soviet intentions after World War II.

The correct answer is (D). The Russian-German Non-Aggression pact was agreed to in 1941 (A). Free trade agreements did not exist during the Cold War (B). The cartoon has nothing to do with admiration of artistic styles (C).

14. What was the most significant response to the focus of this cartoon by the United States and many Western European nations?

    (A) They formed the European Coal and Steel Community and NAFTA.

    (B) They formed NATO (the North Atlantic Treaty Organization).

    (C) They encouraged Eastern European artists to sell their works to the West.

    (D) They built a wall to separate East Germany from West Germany.

    The correct answer is (B). The European Coal and Steel Community was a free-trade agreement between some Western European nations. NAFTA was a trade agreement between the U.S., Canada, and Mexico in the 1990s (A). Choice (C) has no basis in fact.

15. In which conflict did the United Nations authorize and commit troops to oppose forces supported by communist countries?

    (A) Vietnam in the 1950s and 1960s

    (B) Israel in the 1960s

    (C) Korea in the 1950s

    (D) Iraq in the 1990s

    The correct answer is (C), Korea in the 1950s. The United Nations did not authorize the use of its troops in Vietnam (A) or Israel (B). The UN use of force in Iraq was not against communism (D).

How to Tackle the Short-Answer Questions

After your triumphant victory over the multiple-choice section of the exam, you will move on to conquer the four short-answer questions in 50 minutes. Some questions will have stimulus items such as a map or possibly two quotes from historians with different points of view on an important development in history. You will be asked to respond to the question based on your knowledge of world history and on your ability to use those Historical Thinking Skills you have developed.

For each of the four short-answer questions, there are 3 parts: a, b, and c. Each part is worth 1 point. It will help the exam grader (and therefore, yourself) to label your answers a), b), and c) and write *only* the response for that particular question. You don't need a thesis statement; just answer questions a, b, and c *exactly*.

Also, you must write *only inside the box* that is provided for that question. Graders are not allowed to read anything outside the box. If you need a visual clue, picture a text box almost a half page long, with lines inside. You don't have to fill the box, but remember, like the DBQ and the long essay, the short-answer questions are scored based on what you get right, and the wrong stuff is ignored. So write! After you finish the short-answer section, you will have a brief break. Then it's on to the essays.

Here is an example of a short-answer question and response:

Question:

Use the excerpt below and your knowledge of world history to answer all parts of the question that follows.

"[The soldier] stood upon a little mound,
Cast his lethargic eyes around,
And said beneath his breath:
'Whatever happens we have got
The Maxim Gun, and they have not.'
He marked them in their rude advance,
He hushed their rebel cheers;
With one extremely vulgar glance
He broke the Mutineers....
We shot and hanged a few, and then
The rest became devoted men....
While they support us, we should lend
Our every effort to defend,
And from a higher point of view
To give the full direction due
To all the native races."

—Hilaire Belloc, British author and politician,
The Modern Traveler, 1898

a) Briefly explain the historical context of this poem.

b) Describe ONE specific example of native resistance in Africa to the events depicted in this poem.

c) Describe ONE specific example of native resistance in Asia to the events depicted in this poem.

Sample Response

a) The historical context of this poem is 19th century European imperialism of Africa and Asia. Europeans believed themselves to be superior to "natives" and had a right to conquer them. Social Darwinism and strong nationalism fueled this attitude.

b) One example from Africa was when the Zulu warriors attacked British outposts in southern Africa. The Africans won a major battle, but the British were not forced to leave the region.

c) One example from Asia was the Indian Mutiny, or Sepoy Rebellion, when anti-British Indian soldiers fought pro-British Indians and the British army. As in Africa, this rebellion failed to get the British to leave.

Mastering the
Document-Based Question

Your multiple-choice and short-answer sections have been turned in; you've had a short break. Now it's time for you to write two essays: the Document-Based Question (DBQ) and the long-essay question. The DBQ is the first essay you'll encounter, and it is also the most difficult to master. However, thousands of students do well on it—why not you?

The Document-Based Question is just that—a question with documents. Your job is to incorporate the documents and your knowledge of world history into an essay that addresses *all* parts of the question. It is worth 25% of your total score. You will have 55 minutes to write it. The College Board says there will be seven *and only seven* documents.

It's easy to check on your progress as you work through the DBQ and the Long Essay: just above the question are bulleted reminders of the scoring rubric. Check off each bullet as you complete the corresponding task in your essay.

The DBQ is scored on a scale of "dash" to 7. A "dash" score is given to essays that don't even try to address the question. A score of "0" goes to those essays that try to address the question, but earn no points. The scoring rubric is based on a system of 7 points. Few essays earn a "7," so don't worry about that. Just follow these tips, practice, and do your best.

The basic version of the rubric is:

Thesis: 1 point

➤ Essay supports the thesis by showing relationships among the documents (such as similarities or differences): 1 point

➤ Essay correctly uses at least 6 of 7 documents: 1 point

➤ Essay explains Point of View in at least 4 documents: 1 point

➤ Essay places the question in the correct historical context: 1 point (see paragraph 2 below)

➤ Essay uses evidence beyond the documents ("outside information"): 1 point

➤ Essay includes a similar event in another time or place, OR, includes art, literature, or a different field of study such as anthropology in the argument ("synthesis"): 1 point

Test Tip

AP World History exam readers don't start at 7 points and knock off points for mistakes. They start at zero and add points for things you do correctly. They understand that this is a high-pressure exam and that your essay is a first draft. They read beyond your mistakes and assign points based on what you did right.

Mastering the DBQ takes practice. Keep this guide handy to help you through every DBQ you write. **Important:** *In your essay,* **you must use 6 or all 7 of the documents, and include some outside information.** *Name the source* of each document (who created it?) and include point-of-view (POV) (why did they create it? or, how do they know what they're talking about?) to at least 4 documents. (See "E" on page 298.)

FIRST:

Read the question. Pause. Take a deep breath. Read it again, slower this time. Make sure you *understand and underline all the tasks of the question.*

SECOND:

Write down everything that pops into your head from the era of the question. You will use this as a source of outside information in the essay.

Paragraph 1, Thesis: includes 1) all parts of the question with specific examples and 2) three or more *relationships* among the documents based on the prompt of the question. (*Relationships* may support and/or refute the terms of the question.) Thesis can be one or more connected sentences.

Example:

"There were many (*causes and consequences, similarities and differences, factors, responses, effects, issues, etc., depending on the tasks in the question*) in...*repeat the prompt*. For example, (*example 1*) and (*example 2*). The most important is...*pick another example*...because...."

Paragraph 2, Context: Briefly put the topic of the question in historical context.

1.   Define the focus/issue of the question.

2.   What other big social/political/economic/environmental things were happening in the era of the question, or led up to the topic of the question? This information must connect to the question in some way.

Paragraph 3, First Argument Group:

A.   Name this group/argument with a topic sentence that introduces this paragraph;

B.   Use the documents and outside information to address the terms of the question. Tip: The "source" line in the document and the document itself will provide big hints for outside info.

C.   Name the source of each document (who said/wrote it?)

D.   Tell the reader what each document is saying in your own words. Quoting the document is not necessary. (This shows you are "wrestling" with the document—AP readers like that.)

E. Attach point-of-view (POV) to the documents in this group (Why was this document written? In what context? Who is it intended for? How does the author's status affect his/her opinions in this document?)

F. Connect to another era that reflects this topic: "This is similar (*or different*) to the (*name an era*) when. . . ."

Paragraph 4, Second Argument Group (repeat the structure of paragraph 3):

A. Name this group/argument with a topic sentence that introduces this paragraph.

B. Use the documents and use outside information to address the terms of the question. Tip: The "source" line in the document and the document itself will provide big hints for outside info.

C. Name the source of each document (who said/wrote it?)

D. Tell the reader what each document is saying in your own words. Quoting the document is not necessary. (This shows you are "wrestling" with the document—AP readers like that.)

E. Attach point-of-view to the documents in this group (Why was this document written? In what context? Who is it intended for? How does the author's status affect his/her opinions in this document?)

F. Connect to another era that reflects this topic: "This is similar (*or different*) to the (*name an era*) when. . . ."

Paragraph 5, Third Argument Group (repeat the structure of paragraphs 3 and 4):

Remember, the minimum standard is 4 documents for the POV point, but if you attempt explaining the POV in 6 or 7 documents, you leave yourself room to get a couple wrong and still get 4 right.

Paragraph 6, Write a conclusion that includes:

A. All parts of the question; and

B. Three named groups of documents based on the prompt of the question.

   (This will substitute for your opening thesis paragraph in case it is insufficient.)

Be sure you finish your essay with a brief conclusion that addresses all parts of the question. It might count as your thesis if the one at the beginning of your essay falls short.

If you finish your essay ahead of the 55-minute time frame, go back and review your work and make any necessary corrections. Readers understand it's a first-draft essay in a high-pressure situation. If you have extra time, don't waste it—add information, cross stuff out, and rewrite whole paragraphs, if you care to.

Tips on Writing the Long Essay

There are four kinds of long essays that you might see on the AP World History exam. They are: Comparison (similarities and differences), Causation (cause and/or effect), Continuity and Change Over Time, and Periodization, which can be about a turning point in history or a "define the era" question.

On the exam, you are given two long essay prompts, but you only have to write one essay. Both essay questions will be the same type; for example, two Comparison essays. You pick one.

The long essay is graded on a 6-point scale:

➤ thesis (1 point);

➤ address all parts of the question (1 point);

➤ analysis: for example, *why* did something change in history? (1 point);

➤ specific evidence that supports your thesis (1 point for some, 2 points for more);

➤ synthesis: connect a similar event that happened in a different era or place or something from art, literature, society, or economics of the era in question that connects to your discussion (1 point).

The next section includes "how to" guides for success on the AP World History long-essay question. Walk through them one at a time to get comfortable with the requirements for the different types of long-essay questions.

1. **Causation Essay (cause and/or effect of an event or movement)**

   Paragraph 1: State your thesis. "There were many causes (or effects) of (name the event). Causes (or effects) included (name 2). Perhaps the most important cause (or effect) was (name a 3rd cause/effect) because of its (political, social, cultural, environmental or economic) impact on history."

   Paragraph 2: Define the event itself and put it in historical context—*What* was the event? *When* did it happen? *Who* was involved? *What* was its significance?

   Paragraph 3: Discuss as many causes or effects of the event as you can think of. Name the *most* significant cause or effect and tell *why*.

   Paragraph 4: Discuss a similar/different event from another time or place in history. How was that cause (or effect) similar ("This also happened when….") *or* discuss how literature, society, culture, the environment or economics of the era was part of the event.

   Paragraph 5: (2nd chance at thesis) Write a conclusion that summarizes all parts of the question, with specificity, like in your thesis, but worded differently.

2. **Comparison Essay**

   Paragraph 1: State your thesis. "There were many similarities and differences in (name the two things being compared). For example, there were similarities in (provide an example or two) and differences in (provide an example or two). Perhaps the greatest (similarity or difference) was (provide either a similarity or a difference)."

   Paragraph 2: "Perhaps the greatest similarity between (name the 2 things) was _____ because _____. Other similarities include (name as many similarities as you can think of). They were similar because _____."

Paragraph 3: "Perhaps the greatest difference between (name the 2 things) was _____ because _____. Other differences include (discuss as many differences as you can think of). They were different because _____. "

Paragraph 4: Discuss a similar/different event from another time or place in history ("This also happened when….") or discuss how literature, society, culture, the environment or economics of the era was part of the event.

Paragraph 5: (2nd chance at thesis) Conclude with a summary that accurately reflects all the terms of the question, with specificity. In other words, re-write your thesis in another way.

3. Continuity and Change Over Time (CCOT) Essay

Paragraph 1: State your thesis. "There were many continuities and changes in (insert the dates of the question) in (insert all tasks of the question). Continuities included (one specific example) and changes were in (two specific examples)."

Paragraph 2: "Continuities in (insert the terms of the question) in this era included: (discuss as many specific examples you can think of). Perhaps the most important continuity was _____ because_____. These remained the same over time because _____." Provide as many relevant examples as possible.

Paragraph 3: "Changes in (insert all tasks of the question) in this era included: (discuss as many specific examples you can think of). Perhaps the greatest change was_____ because_____. These changed over time because _____." Provide as many relevant examples as possible.

Paragraph 4: Discuss an event from another time or place in history that also changed or stayed the same or discuss how another field (e.g., literature, art, politics, society, religion, economics) of the era reflects a similarity or change that's in your essay already.

Paragraph 5: (2nd chance at thesis) Conclude with a summary that accurately reflects all the terms of the question, with specificity. In other words, re-write your thesis in another way.

4. Periodization (Turning Point) Essay

This essay is a combination of CCOT and Comparison question. The basic structure of this essay is: society/government, etc., was like *this* until a *turning point* happened, and then society/government, etc., changed to *that*. Why did they change? But some things remained the same from one era to the next. Why did those continue?

Paragraph 1: State your thesis. "There were many reasons why *the topic of the question* (for example, a war) changed (society, government, etc.). Some of these reasons were (a and b) but the greatest reason was (c). However, some things persisted, such as (d)." Include one sentence defining the turning point.

Paragraph 2: Set the stage before the turning point. What was (society, politics, economics, the environment—whatever *the terms of the question* are) like in the era just before? Link your examples only to the terms of the question. Provide as many specific examples as you can.

Paragraph 3: Discuss the turning point. What was it? *How* did it lead to changes in the next era? *What* was the greatest change from one era to the next? *Why?*

Paragraph 4: What persisted from one era to the next? Provide as many examples as you can think of. Why did some things persist? How did art or literature of the era reflect changes or continuities between the eras? In what ways were these processes similar in another era in history?

Paragraph 5: (2nd chance at Thesis) Conclude with a summary that accurately reflects all the terms of the question, with specificity. In other words, re-write your thesis in another way.

5. Periodization ("Define the Era") Essay

Like the "Turning Point" essay, this is also a CCOT and Comparison question at the same time. The essay prompt will include an era—let's say the Industrial Revolution. Discuss features that support the idea that there really was a revolution, and features that *didn't* change, in other words, what wasn't so revolutionary about this era. Pick a side: do you agree or not agree with the label of the era? *Why?*

Paragraph 1: State your thesis. "There were many reasons why (the era of the question) is correctly named. For example: (cite two examples), and the greatest reason why this era is aptly named is____. However, one could argue that this label is incorrect because _____. "

Paragraph 2: Provide a definition of the era and include why most historians think it is labeled as such.

Paragraph 3: Discuss the era of the question. Provide as many examples as you can think of that support the idea that this era is correctly labeled. Which example *most* supports the label of the era? *Why?*

Paragraph 4: What evidence counters the idea that the era is correctly labeled? How did art or literature of the era reflect or counter the name of the era? Or what would be a better era for the label to fit?

Paragraph 5: (2nd chance at Thesis) Conclude with a summary that accurately reflects all the terms of the question, with specificity. In other words, re-write your thesis in another way.

Countdown Calendar

Here's a countdown calendar of preparation tips for the AP World History exam.

SIX WEEKS BEFORE THE EXAM

➤ Read this book cover to cover and pay attention to its advice. Remember always to keep the big picture of AP World History's themes in mind.

➤ Go to *www.rea.com/studycenter* and take the free online practice exam to find out where your strengths and weaknesses lie. Focus your remaining study time on your weaker areas.

➤ Find previously released AP World History essay questions and write, write, write. Keep in mind that released exams before 2016 are not the same format as 2017 and later. Use the older ones as a guide to essay topics.

FOUR WEEKS BEFORE THE EXAM

➤ Review your study materials every night to keep the material and skills fresh in your mind. Pay special attention to Parts I and II of this book to increase and sharpen your content knowledge.

TWO WEEKS BEFORE THE EXAM

➤ Quiz yourself on the rubrics for each essay and commit them to memory.

➤ Review your study materials every night to keep the material and skills fresh in your mind, adding Part III to your continued study of Parts I and II.

ONE DAY BEFORE THE EXAM

➤ Reread Chapter 1 of this *Crash Course* and then get a good night's sleep—at least 8 hours. If you've paid close attention to the advice in this book, relax. You are prepared for success! It's important to wake up fresh in the morning.

THE DAY OF THE EXAM

➤ Take a shower and put on clothes. Don't laugh, some people get really nervous! Not you, though. You've been studying this book.

➤ Plan to show up at the exam site at least 20 minutes before the scheduled start time for the exam.

➤ Bring two fresh No. 2 pencils with clean erasers and two working blue- or black-ink pens.

➤ Bring a snack and a bottle of water for the break after the short-answer questions.

➤ Be prepared to turn in your cell phone and other electronic devices at the beginning of the exam.

➤ The exam proctor will read a lot of instructions—be patient.
  Plan to spend about 4 hours at the exam site.

➤ Answer every multiple-choice question, even if you have to
  guess, and all parts of each essay.

➤ When you're done, treat yourself to some fun time with friends.
  There's probably a blockbuster movie that just came out.

Notes